MORNING LIGHT

LIGHT

SECRETS FOR BREAKTHROUGH IN PRAYER

Donna Sundberg

Donna Sundberg

ISBN-10: 1795207779
ISBN-13: 978-1795207775

Scriptural Support

1 Tim. 2: 1 & 2
"First of all, that supplications, prayers, **intercessions** and giving of thanks be made for all men, for kings and all who are in authority, that we may lead a quiet and peaceable life in all godliness and reverence; for this is good and acceptable in the sight of God our savior, who desires all men to be saved and come to the knowledge of the truth."

Jeremiah 9:17, 18
"Call for the women (*those who will suffer and agonize in prayer*) that they may come; and send for the wailing women (*those who will cry out for the sins of a nation.*) Let them make haste and take up a wailing for us, that our eyes may shed tears and our eyelids flow with water"

Psalms 30:5
"For His anger endureth but for a moment, in His favor is life: weeping may endure for a night, but joy cometh in the morning."

Galatians 4:19
"My little children, of whom I travail in birth again until Christ be formed in you"

Proverbs 13:12 & 19b
"Hope deferred maketh the heart sick: but when the desire cometh it is a tree of life" "A desire accomplished is sweet to the Soul"

Contents

PREFACE

The inspiration for writing this book originally came out of a lot of trouble and confusion in my own personal life. I began to identify with people in the Bible that had a plethora of problems and had suffered many losses. *Crisis* and *Confusion* surrounded my family much of the time. In my search to find out why we were experiencing so many problems, even though I didn't get any clear answers right away, I began to recognize that I had a void in my heart that no matter how much I tried to ignore it, the stronger it became. Although I carried the label of "Christian", I really didn't know Father God and felt powerless to change any of my situations. I would try to pray, but my prayers seemed to go only as high as the ceiling, which of course left me feeling empty and hopeless. As I faced the cold hard facts about my life I realized that I was on a journey that I was totally unprepared to undertake.

My friends in the health club where I taught Aerobics invited me to a few Christian Women's functions where they talked a lot about the Holy Spirit; a subject that was never really discussed much less taught about in my spiritual upbringing. My hunger began to be stoked; I wanted more of God and nothing was going to change that; but the more I heard, the more I was increasingly disillusioned with the brand of Christianity I was raised with and I knew uncomfortable changes were upon my horizon.

Marriage, divorce and remarriage, along with dealing with my own dysfunction and abuse from my past, brought a lot of emotional trauma; not only for me, but also for my children.

As I began to really press into the Scriptures I found the answer I was looking for; *an encounter with Jesus Christ.*

It was at that time, I found out that a Messianic Jewish woman, who later became my friend, was sent to my aerobics class to *secretly* pray for my salvation and encounter with Jesus Christ! She was on an assignment from God and I didn't even know it! Months later, I got born again and a whole new perspective of God and *heaven* came alive in me!

God brought me to His feet and began teaching me, with the help of His Spirit, how to pray effectively. When I started searching in the Word of God to learn how to pray, I was overwhelmed; the Bible taught so many different ways to pray! For instance, there was the prayer of faith, the prayer of agreement, the prayer of supplication, the prayer of importunity, the prayer of consecration, etc.! Overload! Eventually though, through consistent study of the Word of God and some help from my pastors along the way, I learned to pray by trial and error, all the while believing God for restoration in my personal crises.

The truths I'm going to share throughout this book did not come easy. There were *mysteries* to be revealed and divine *secrets* to be gleaned that once I was able to grasp them, helped me *breakthrough* in prayer. I learned for instance about the power of the blood of Jesus (*Exodus 12*), that when applied to the doorpost of the Israelites homes, was able to deliver an entire nation from the hands of Pharaoh. There was also one woman named Rahab that received salvation for her entire household (*including her property and her animals*) by simply hanging a replica of the blood, a scarlet thread, in her window. (*Joshua 6:17*) I was especially interested in her when I found out that she was an outsider to the promises of God at the time the offer was made. God saved her and her entire family from destruction because her faith was in the blood of a slain lamb. I also learned that prayer was not a formula but a yielding to the Holy Spirit, our most valuable prayer partner in life's battles. This *partner* would even teach us how to pray to get *breakthroughs* when it seemed it wasn't going to happen.

It was during those troubled yet amazing times that God revealed His extraordinary and unremitting love for me and my dysfunctional household and wanted nothing but good things for us. As I came out of my pain and saw the wonderful answers to *prayer* and in particular, the prayers of *intercession*, I realized that others were suffering through many similar *crisis situations*, but didn't know how to pray or know the price that needed to be paid in prayer for many situations to turn around. I wish I could say at this point that the changes happened quickly, but they didn't. I had to learn to stick it out with God and eventually things began to turn around.

As I grew in the knowledge of all the different kinds of prayer, I realized that the *prayer of intercession* was the least understood in the church at that time, along with *travail* or *birthing* prayers (*our key topics on prayer in this book*). Even though Paul encouraged Timothy to pray the prayers of *intercession*, very few people in my circle were regularly engaged in it; mostly due to a lack of understanding or fear. The same was true of *travail* or *birthing prayers*. God showed me that there were special times in the history of His dealings with the children of Israel that this kind of praying was needed and that it is still needed today. A couple of His Prophets even called for the women to come and pray and co-labor with Him in order for His will to be accomplished. These times were usually *crisis* times, though not limited just to those times, but had to be done immediately and consistently until the job was finished; which clearly defines what true *intercession* is all about.

As I studied I found Scriptures to help me understand more about the prayer of *intercession*. I had read that Jesus *"ever lived to make intercession for us"* but was unclear how He was doing that from where He was seated! I didn't know that in that *aspect* of intercession, we had to join Him in *prayer* and when we do, we become *"intercessors"*.

While the hour is late, I believe we can still redeem the time as we learn more about prayer in an intercessory capacity!

One

Prophetic Urgency

In the late 90's, a good while after I had learned the principles of *intercession* through study and practice, and had seen some powerful things God did through my prayers, I was awakened one night by the Holy Spirit with such urgency that I immediately sat up in the bed wondering what horrific thing had just happened! I quietly got out of the bed as to not wake my husband and quickly ran down to the basement bedroom where I normally prayed. God instructed me to read <u>Genesis 18:16</u>. In that passage of Scripture God went to visit Abraham and wanted to talk to him about two important events. One was the birth of Isaac and the other was about the judgment of Sodom and Gomorrah that was about to take place. I really didn't understand what He was showing me at first, but as I reflected on it, I began to get more revelation. He reminded me of a Scripture that brought some clarity.

<u>Amos 3:4</u>
"Surely, the Lord God does nothing unless He reveals His *secret* counsel to His servants the prophets."

This told me that God wants those of us who are in Covenant with Him to be prepared for what He's going to do in each generation before He actually does it. Notice it says "He reveals His *secret counsel* to His servants". (*A Secret to Breakthrough*) In other words, He would reveal things to his servants that "were not going to be made known to others". This definitely got my attention. God was talking to me! I had an uneasy feeling that He was speaking to me about the latter of the two events mentioned! I knew from previous studies that Sodom and Gomorrah were two cities that suffered great judgment because of their sins.

In Kevin J. Conner's Book, <u>Interpreting the Symbols and Types</u>, He said that the city of Sodom was a symbol of Immorality and Vileness and the city of Gomorrah, was a symbol of Idolatry, Pride, Idleness and Prosperity.

As I revisited those passages of Scripture, I realized that God was warning Abraham of impending destruction that was coming to those cities because of their gross sins. I learned that God has reasons why He reveals things to us. In this case, it was because Lot, Abraham's nephew and his family lived in one of the cities targeted for destruction. As I thought about it more, I realized that Father God was showing me that He was concerned about *my family members*, and wanted me to engage in *intercessory* prayer for them! I had grown tired and despondent in some cases when it came to prayer; the more I prayed, the further away the promises seemed, so I gave up. I didn't know that *endurance* was part of the process and sometimes that could take years! (*A Secret to Breakthrough*) I later learned this is known as "backlash" from our enemy the devil. I had fallen *asleep* and had *not completed* some very important prayer assignments. I began to cry and I repented for all of the times I had not obeyed Him in those assignments. Thank you God for *waking* me up and re-invigorating me to pray for my family and pray I did!

The Encounter Enlarges
A National Crisis

During the following months, I remained very troubled in my heart, but as I pursued Him for answers I received more revelation; the plight of our nation as well as the plight of God's very own people, the Church! The burden was larger than I could have ever imagined. He began to lead me in the direction of *corporate correction* and *chastisements* for our sins. The Lord opened my eyes to let me see how Israel suffered in the wilderness because of their continual sin and backslidings, and how they had to endure severe *chastisements* for ignoring God's correction. He had sent His prophets to warn them but they wouldn't listen. I began to understand that if we continued to ignore the warnings of His prophets, we as a nation would experience some of the same things Israel had gone through. (*1 Cor. 10*)

He showed me that we are allowing some of the same sins in our day that provoked God's divine correction (*judgments/chastisements*) of yesterday. He spoke to my heart and said that even though He had looked upon this nation in times past with grace and favor because of the righteous, He would not be able to continue to do so unless His people would come back to Him fully and offer up true repentance and prayers. He also showed me that the Church in America, for the most part, was *asleep* (*just like I had been*) and at "ease in Zion" and was totally unaware of the dangers that were lurking in the shadows.

As I continued to meditate on these things in my heart, I began to hear similar "prophetic voices" like those in the Bible, all over our nation and realized that the Lord was speaking to me not only about *intercessory prayer* for my *family* but also for prayers for the people of God to return to their God, and reposition themselves to offer up prayers for this *nation*. He put it upon my heart to organize prayer gatherings and focus on teaching on prayer and get His people praying again! Our nation was rotting from within for many reasons and the church was *asleep,* but God had a plan! His desire was to use His church to turn things around, but in order to do that, He had to pass her through some fire! I wasn't totally sure what all that meant, but I trusted God to show me.

I continued gathering groups of people for prayer and having prophetic conferences, etc. to let the people know what I had heard from the Lord. More dreams of very significant events kept coming to me and I knew God was moving. Little did I know we would be moving also - literally! In the year 2000 my husband and I made a geographical change and moved us from Colby, KS to Seminole, a small town in Oklahoma, to pastor another church.

Once there, I followed the same instructions God had given me; only this time the crowds were not as receptive to the Prophetic Call to Prayer! My husband asked me to lead prayer every Sunday morning before the services and even though many would come, there were just as many who opposed it. I found out that a call to prayer is always strongly opposed if people's hearts are not right with God! A prevailing lack of understanding usually provokes people to be mean and critical and I firmly believe it is out of fear. SELAH.

As the Holy Spirit would move on us we would begin to weep and fall on our faces before God, asking Him to have mercy on us. The elders began to tell my husband that I was only scaring the people as I wept for the nation in our prayer gatherings and asked for prayer to be stopped! We had already grown to about 45 - 50 people praying at the altar before the services! Of course we didn't stop! We had to press in for *breakthrough*. Who knew resistance would come from within!

On Sunday morning 09/09/2001, the Sunday before 911, we had gathered as usual before the AM service started and all of us began to respond to a sovereign move of God as we wept in repentance and cried out for mercy. It was as if we all knew that there was such a darkness looming over our nation and that the outcome would be devastating, even though we knew that God would help us through this.

None of us could rest after that service and none of us could have ever imagined how bad it was actually going to be.

That Tuesday 911 happened. People were shocked! My husband and I immediately prayed about canceling our first Women's Conference at that church. The Lord had impressed me to entitle it, "The Fire Intensifies" and it was quite an eye opening revelation! It was scheduled to begin on Thursday of that week. He told us not to cancel. I thought the people scheduled to come would all cancel, but I was surprised that it was one of the largest conferences I have ever had. They came from everywhere! Many people were numb and perplexed and looking for answers. I taught on the Secret Place and how at this time we all needed to find it and hear what our God would say to us. In their shock and grief, many asked why God had let this happen. For days, the media interviewed many preachers who said it was *judgment* for our sins and others said it was *persecution*. That was really disturbing to me because we as the church in our nation should have had agreement in our answers! This made many people fearful and afraid and didn't know what voices to trust. Those were very unstable times for us as

Christians and many were not consoled. We needed stabilizing, but for the most part, confusion ensued.

<u>Isaiah 33:6</u>
"And wisdom and knowledge shall be the stability of thy times and strength of salvation; the fear of the LORD is his treasure."

What a promise! Wisdom, knowledge and the fear of the Lord would have stabilized us had we been unified in our pursuit of finding answers from God. I believe the majority of church leaders as a whole missed a great opportunity to come together for the sole purpose of pursuing God for answers. Instead, all we heard were contradictions of one another's assessments of the situation which brought more fear and confusion. Here we are 18 years later at this book's printing, and not much appears to have changed; but I can assure you by the Spirit, there's been spiritual progress! There's a remnant of God's people who have heard from heaven and have entered the great conflict in "intercession" praying for mercy and the will and purpose of God to be fulfilled. I believe we are in one of the biggest battles for the soul of our nation and I believe we will see God do many signs and wonders as we unite in prayer to turn our nation back to God and honor His ways.

Just like Jeremiah and Abraham, true Believers should be close enough to God to hear both *blessings* and *warnings* from the Holy Spirit. Unfortunately, those who had truly heard from God long before 911, heard the *warnings* and spoke them out but were written off and accused of being too hard and judgmental along with being labeled as false prophets; yours truly included. Maybe they *were* sounding judgmental and hard in their zeal in comparison to the fluff that that was being regularly preached for decades, but those who heard and turned their lives around began to hear the same things! As the Spirit would say to all of us, "He that hath an ear, (*spiritual ear*) let Him hear what the Spirit is saying." (*Rev. 2:7*)

I believe we could all agree that the church and the nation are in *crisis* and needs a season of repentance and prayer. Even though we now have a president that is literally becoming a voice for us as Christians and is working to overturn a lot of the anti-Christian decisions made by the last president (s), we are still facing severe consequences on a corporate level for our sins.

Our greatest need at present is for the Church to return to God with its whole heart and engage in intercessory prayer for our nation and its leaders. (*1 Tim. 2: 1 & 2*) We need a *revival* that is genuine and a *reformation* that transforms completely the existing state of affairs on both fronts! As we will see in the chapters to follow, we have been weakened because of our corporate sins across the board – and must turn around!

Before we faint from fear and trepidation caused by this "reality check", and there's more, I have found some good news for people who are in crisis, and for all of us that I hope you remember as you read this book!

<u>Ezra 9:8</u>
"And now for a little while grace has been shown from the Lord our God, to leave us a *remnant* to escape, (*judgment*) and to give us a peg in His holy place that our God may enlighten our eyes and give us a measure of *revival* in our bondage."

Remnant - *Heb. Peleytah* - escape, deliverance; a small portion of people who have escaped judgment and who live for God

<u>Jeremiah 7:3</u>
"This is what the Lord Almighty, the God of Israel says:
'*Reform* your ways and actions, and I will let you live
(*experience God's blessings*) in this place.'"

Revival - *Heb. Michyah* - preservation of life (*zoe*); quickening; recovery

Reform – *Heb.* – *Yatab* – amends; make well, better, pleasing

God is calling men and women everywhere to not only pray but to understand how to use His power in an *intercessory* capacity. We become powerful weapons against the darkness that is holding this nation as well as God's people in captivity!

Two

First Things First

In this passage of Scripture we can see that prayer is a priority on God's agenda and it's not just for our family members, but for all groups of people.

1 Tim. 2: 1 & 2
"First of all, that supplications, prayers, *intercessions* and giving of thanks be made for all men, for kings and all who are in authority, that we may lead a quiet and peaceable life in all godliness and reverence; for this is good and acceptable in the sight of God our savior, who desires all men to be saved and come to the knowledge of the truth."

Priority - *Webster's* - superiority in rank, position or privilege; something given or meriting attention before competing alternatives

Notice the reasons Paul gave Timothy this priority; to assure a way to preach the gospel unhindered; prayers for men to be saved; and for all leaders of civil government, including our church leaders. When Paul says *all men* he means *all men*. Why pray for all these people - so the Kingdom of God can expand and for *peace* to prevail in our land.

If we look around today, we'll definitely notice that the battle is raging and there is not much peace. We must not quit! The word of God says that "men ought to always pray, and not faint . . ." (*Luke 18:1*) Why?

The book of Galatians tells us "in due season we will reap if we faint not." (*Gal. 6:9*)

Faint – Gr. *Ekkakeo* – to be wearied out or exhausted.

Reap – Gr. *Therizo* – receive a harvest; pertaining to sowing and reaping

Many would agree that the church and the nation are so far away from God that we can't really see our true spiritual condition. The further away we move from Him, the more deceived we become. We are then recognized by God as being *backslidden*.

God spoke to the prophet Jeremiah about Israel's *backslidden* condition saying, "Your dwelling place is in the midst of deceit; through deceit they refuse to know me." (*Jeremiah 9:6*)

In the book of Ezekiel things had gotten so bad that they couldn't tell the difference between the "holy and the profane"; if it feels good and you judge it to be right, go ahead and do it! Forget about the consequences that follow people who break the laws of God.

I had to get to a place in my life that I realized the reasons for all the desolation and destruction in my house was because of my sins and the sins of those I was associated with. Unfortunately, deception was a huge part of the scenario, both at home and at church! I had to repent of my sins and be separated from things that would pull me away from my relationship with Jesus Christ.

To add insult to injury, I found out that many of the churches I had attended were being led by people who were falling into gross deceptions and were struggling with sin themselves; some were so serious that they even lost their Pastorates! High profile flogging is what it looked like on television! It was so disturbing. The consequences: churches became "weak and powerless", "sport to unbelievers" and "a laughing stock" to other nations.

A comprehensive study of the Old Testament reveals to us what brought God's corporate *judgments/divine chastisements* to the people of God.

1. Shedding of Innocent Blood
2. Sexual Perversion
3. Idolatry
4. Broken Covenants

We must not kid ourselves. I believe all of our woes are caused by our participation in those sins and the further we move away from God and His ways, the more deception leads us astray into destruction! Because of our corporate sins, our perception of God has been altered. We assume that God doesn't notice these things and because we have the "Christian" label tacked onto our identity as a nation, we are somehow going to be exempt from any sort of extreme *consequences*. Quite the opposite is true. One of the basic laws of God is "we reap what we sow". God gives the greater accountability to those who profess to know Him! SELAH

Consequences –Gr. *Adikeo* – results of wrong doing; penalty for unjust actions

The Cost of Deception

Let's look at some stats and see what *deception* has done to us over the last few generations.

As we look at the above grouping of sins that offended God and brought serious and sometimes very severe *consequences/chastisements* we can far better understand that this is also *our* condition at present.

Chastisement/Punishment – *Hebrew* – *yacar* - to chasten; discipline; instruct; admonish; reform; improve...*Strong's* - to chastise literally (*with blows*) or figuratively (*with words*)

I believe our ignorance of God and His ways and our departure from His Covenant has severely cost us. Instead of going from glory to glory as the Scriptures say, we go from *crisis to crisis*! Being self deceived because we have chosen the *abridged* version of Christianity has really robbed us of our true spiritual blessings. If we will open our spiritual eyes, we will see that too many of us and our children are *broken* and have been *asleep* for many generations!

Abridged - *Webster's* - to shorten by omission of words without sacrifice of sense; Condense; to shorten in duration or extent; formally, to reduce in scope; diminish (*to lessen the authority, dignity or reputation of something*); to gradually become less important.

Is this what has caused us all this trouble? Yes! Look around and you and I can see the fruit of our ways collectively.

Alcoholism, abortion on demand, drug addiction, and divorce; also infidelity in marriages, sexual and physical abuse and perversion have left many of us emotionally crippled, empty, and angry and confused. I believe our children rebel because they are confused and disappointed from an early age because they have been conditioned through our lack of real spirituality and see no hope for their future. God intentionally made our human spirit strong for the purpose of standing on what we believe, but without a working knowledge of God and His ways, we tend to believe things contrary to what God says is best for us. Given our own choices we stumble and fall prey to all sorts of weird concepts, and in frustration run to a form of "pseudo" peace through the use of drugs, alcohol, and even false religions. The enemy definitely has his foot in the door of our nation and the church. I believe because of it many people are suffering from a condition known as Hope *Deferred* because they have given up. SELAH

<u>*Proverbs 13:12*</u>
"Hope deferred makes the heart sick; but when the desire comes, it is a tree of life."

Hope – *Webster's* – to desire with expectation; to expect with confidence; a hopeful expectation for good (*More on this later*)

As a Biblical counselor for over fifteen (15) years, this was definitely the spiritual climate I worked in. Many who do not know God or have walked away from Him for whatever reasons were in this condition. Others were "asleep" or totally unaware of the presence of God or of the spiritual darkness that had taken over their lives. That was me for a long time! God had even given me spiritual dreams about some of the dangers my children and I were facing, but I was *asleep* (*spiritually unaware*) and didn't know how to interpret what He was saying. Like many of these that came to me, I had drifted away from God without even realizing it. I had quit praying because of disappointment and trials, and was now trying to do things on my own without realizing that I had to make my way back to God *first*. That's the self deception Jeremiah the Prophet was talking about as we'll see later in this chapter.

This is the revelation I believe Jeremiah received when he saw the true spiritual condition of the people of God in His day. They had taken themselves out from under the Covenant of Promise and were walking in deception. He was heartbroken because he clearly saw their demise.

<u>Jeremiah 8:22 – 23</u>
For the hurt of the daughter of my people am I hurt; I am black; astonishment hath taken hold on me. Is there no balm in Gilead; is there no physician there? Why then is *not* the health of the daughter of my people recovered.

They were spiritually sick and it appeared that it would be a while before they could be healed because they didn't want to turn back to God. God even made them a really good offer, but they were so deceived, they had the nerve to refuse Him!

<u>Jeremiah 6:16</u>
Thus says the Lord,
"Stand in the way and see, and ask for the Old Paths, where the good way is, and walk in it, Then you will find rest for your souls.
But they said, "We will not walk in it".

I couldn't believe this when I read it. Now I totally understand why Jeremiah was so saddened with grief over their condition. It is very sad to say this, but I believe many of us have entered the same path as these did in that day and are suffering severely for it; but it can get better.

Depression

(1) 1 out of 10 people suffers with depression & 80% never seek treatment or counseling.

(2) 32,000,000 currently suffer with depression and anxiety disorders. (2016 Census Bureau)

(3) 1 out of 8 will require special treatment or assistance

(4) Adolescent depression is on the rise. Depression strikes people of all ages; even as young as 6 years of age.

(5) Depression and anxiety disorders cost the U.S. more than $42 billion a year, almost 1/3 of our $148 billion total mental health bill (according to "The Economic Burden of Anxiety Disorders"

(6) Depression is defined as a state of "*hopelessness*".

(7) Victims of depression lose all sense of perception of self, God and life.

(8) Depressed people should never be overlooked as it is a precursor to suicide.

Quote: Norman Wright's book, Crisis Counseling, - "Depression is like a set of camera filters that focus upon the darker portions of life and take away the *Warmth, Action* and *Joy* from the scene"

(Some of these stats taken from: Depression and Bipolar Support Alliance (DBSA)

Divorce

(1) Marital separation and divorce are major causes of depression among young people.
(2) 51% of all professing Christians/Non Christian marriages end in divorce.
(3) 45%of all children will live with one (1) parent before they reach the age of 18.
(4) 12 Million Children under the age of 18 have parents who are divorced.
(5) The highest rate of adolescent suicide is among children of divorce.
(6) 2 out of 3 will commit suicide. (Taken from Newsweek)
(7) Depression, confusion, anger and hopelessness are major factors involved in children and teenagers using drugs and alcohol as a form of self-medicating.

Note:

Many of the stats I have read say that the divorce rates are going down in Christian marriages; but we are still dealing with the damages from divorce over the past 3 or 4 decades when divorce rates were at their highest; rebellion against God, multiple marriages, children living in broken homes, loss of parental guidance, drug and alcohol use, etc.

Suicide

(1) Approx. 44,000 people commit suicide in the U.S. per year. Estimates indicate at least 5 million attempted suicides per year.
(2) For every 25 suicides, there were at least twenty-five 25 more attempts.

(3) ½ million people commit suicide worldwide.

(4) In the 15 to 19 yr. old group, suicide is the 3rd cause of death next to accidents and cancer.

(5) In the 65 yr. old group, it is the number one leading cause of death in men. (38 per 100,000)

(6) Suicide is the 10th leading cause of death in the U.S. (Taken from National Center for Injury Prevention and Control)

(7) 25% commit suicide under psychiatric care confined to hospitals.

(8) 40% commit suicide on an impulse during a period of emotional upset; includes stress, pain, defeat, bullying, etc.

(Stats taken from the American Foundation for Suicide Prevention)

Abuse - Sexual & Physical – Adults

(1) Abuse can happen to anyone, regardless of age, race, religious beliefs, education, or marital status.

(2) One Hundred percent (100%) of physical abuse starts with emotional abuse

(3) One in 3 *women* and one in 4 *men* have experienced rape, physical violence or some form of severe stalking by an intimate partner in their lifetime.

(4) On average, 24 people per minute are victims of rape, physical violence by an intimate partner in the U.S; more than 12 million men and women per year.

(5) Over 3 women are beaten every 15 seconds.

(6) Battering is the single major cause of injury to women in the U.S.

(7) Twenty (20%) of all hospital emergency room visits by women are attributed to wife beating.

(8) Seventy percent (70%) of all emergency room assault cases are women.

(9) Four thousand (4,000) women die each year as a result of beatings, more than auto accidents, muggings, rapes and strangers combined.

(10) Fifty percent (50%) of female deaths are caused by the man who said "until death do us part".

(11) Seventy-five percent (75%) of female related homicides from domestic violence happen after a woman leaves her abuser.

(12) In every home where there is an abused spouse, there are abused children also.
(Some of these stats were taken from the book, The Courage to Say No More by Traci Kemble; Center for the Prevention of Domestic Abuse)

Abuse - Sexual & Physical - Children

(1) A report of child abuse is made every 10 seconds!

(2) One in 3 girls and one in 7 boys will be sexually assaulted by the age of 18.

(3) More than 4 children die each day because of child abuse.

(4) More than 90% of child sexual abuse victims know their attackers.

(5) Seventy percent (70%) of children that die from abuse are under the age of 4.

(6) About 30% of abused/neglected children will abuse.

(7) The estimated annual cost of child abuse and neglect is $124 Billion.
(Stats taken from DOJ; American Society for the Positive Care of Children; U.S. Department of Health and Human Services; Sexual Assault as Reported to Law Enforcement by Howard Snyder;

Alcoholism

(1) There are over seventeen 17 million confirmed alcoholics in this country.

(2) Alcohol abuse contributes to more than 88,000 deaths per year and over $120,000,000,000 in economic losses.

(3) Over 28 million adults grew up with an alcoholic parent.

(4) Over 623,000 youth ages 12 – 17 have AUD (Alcohol Use Disorder) in 2015.

(5) Alcoholism is implicated in the development of throat cancer, heart disease, cirrhosis of the liver and mental deterioration, among other serious conditions.

(6) Most *medical doctors* agree that is is very difficult and almost impossible to combat alcoholism without outside medical and spiritual assistance.

(7) More than ten percent 10% of U.S. children live with a parent with alcohol problems.

(Some of these stats were taken from Children of Alcoholism *by Judith S. Seixas & Geraldine Youcha; National Institute on Alcoholism)*

Teen Sex/Pregnancies/Sexually Transmitted Diseases

(1) The U.S. has the highest teen pregnancy rate of the Western industrialized world.

(2) 1 in 5 young people have sex before the age of 17.

(3) Most young people begin having sex in their mid-to-late teens, about 8 years before they marry; more than ½ of 17-year olds have had intercourse.

(4) While 93% of teenage women report that their first intercourse was voluntary, 1/4 of these young women report that it was unwanted.

(5) One (1) million teens become pregnant each year.

(6) Thirteen percent (13%) of all U.S. births are to teens.

(7) Seventy-eight percent (78%) of births to teens occur outside of marriage.

(8) A sexually active teenager who does not use contraceptives has a 90% chance of becoming pregnant within one year.

(9) Every year 3 million teens – about 1 in 4 sexually experienced teens – acquire an STD. *(Sexually Transmitted Disease)*

(10) Twenty million (20,000,000) new sexually transmitted diseases are reported in youths ages 15 to 24. This takes up ¼ of the sexually active population in the U.S.

(11) In a single act of unprotected sex with an infected partner, a teenage woman has a 1% risk of acquiring HIV, a 30% risk of getting genital herpes and a 50% chance of contracting gonorrhea.

(12) Chlamydia, gonorrhea, syphilis reported in 2015 reached the highest number ever in the U.S. 1.5 million Chlamydia cases reported; four 400,000 cases of gonorrhea, and nearly 240,000 cases of primary and secondary syphilis – the most infectious stages of the disease.

(13) Chlamydia, gonorrhea and viral hepatitis are more common among teens than among older men and women.

(14) Teens have higher rates of gonorrhea than do sexually active men and women aged 20 to 44.

(15) In some studies, up to 15% of sexually active teenage women have been found to be infected with the human Papillomavirus, many with a strain of the virus linked to cervical cancer.

(16) Teenage women have a higher hospitalization rate than older women for acute pelvic inflammatory disease (PID), which can lead to infertility & ectopic pregnancy.

(Stats from The Alan Guttmacher Institute - Revised 9/1999; American Center for Disease Control and Prevention, 2015-16 report)

Abortion

(1) Nearly fifty-eight 58.5 million babies have been aborted since Roe V Wade decision legalized abortion in the United States. (*A report from National Right to Life 2015*)

(2) There are some 44% of women who have repeat abortions as a form of birth control

(3) Approximately 3,300 to 4,400 babies are aborted every day.

(4) Eighty-eight percent (88%) of the women interviewed said they were coerced by husbands, boyfriends or parents.

(5) Thirty percent (30%) of all abortions are done to teens.

(These stats were taken from *Stat from Alan Guttmacher Institute Updated* - Facts in Brief; some stats taken from a letter from Stan Clark, a senator from the 40th District of the State of Kansas; National Right to Life;

Drug Addiction

(1) There were approximately 20.6 million people in the United States over the age of 12 with an addiction in 2011.

(2) Over 23 million people are addicted to both drugs/alcohol.

(3) Over 100 people die every day of overdose of drugs.

(4) The rate has tripled in 20 years.

(5) Approx 7 million people with an addiction also suffer with mental illness

(6) Over 90% of those with an addiction began drinking, smoking or using illicit drugs before the age of 18.

(7) The number of those using heroin has tripled over the last 16 years.

(8) The preliminary figures from the National Center for Health Statistics suggest that there were more than 64,000 drug overdose deaths in 2016. A shocking report reveals that synthetic opiates like fentanyl overtook both heroin and prescription painkillers in terms of overdose deaths.

(9) It is estimated that 80% of new hepatitis C infections occur among those who use drugs intravenously.

(10) Nearly half of those who use heroin reportedly started abusing prescription pain killers before they ever used heroin.

(11) Over a quarter million of drug-related emergency room visits are related to heroin abuse.

(12) There were over 65 million opiate deaths in the year 2016

(13) Rates of illicit drug use are highest among those aged 18 to 25.

(14) The sale of prescription painkillers has increased by over 300% since 1999.

(15) Almost 3 out of 4 prescription overdoses are caused by painkillers.

(16) Tens of millions of Americans use prescription medications non-medically ea. year.

(www.drugabuse.gove/pulications/drugfacts/treatment)

Pornography

(1) A staggering 40 million people have visited porn sites on the internet

(2) The pornography business estimates 12 Billion dollars in the U.S. annually

(3) The average age of a first internet porn experience is 11 years old.

(4) Largest consumer of Internet pornography is 12 – 17 years old age group

(5) U.S. Porn revenues exceeds the combined revenues of ABC, NBC, and CBS $6.2 Billion

(6) Child pornography generates $3 Billion annually

(7) Pornography increased marital infidelity by 300%

(8) The most common female role in pornography is women in their 20's portraying Teens

(9) Recorded child sexual exploitation (known as child porn) is one of the fastest growing on-line businesses.

(10) 64% of young people, ages 13-24 actively seek out porn weekly

(11) 624,000 + child pornography traders have been discovered on line in the U.S.

(12) At least 30% of all data transferred across the internet is pornography related.

(Taken from: Web root; Huffington Post; John Millward, personal research team; IWF; IJ)

I know these stats are pretty rough, but we have to recognize that these numbers represent how far we've come from the old paths and the good ways that were offered by God to the people in Jeremiah's day and what Jesus Christ offers today. Please keep in mind that these stats include believers and non-believers alike. These are consequences for sins that have reached a corporate level and have been perpetuated for many generations. I believe we have offended God so badly, that mercy from Him is the only thing that will save us from being destroyed as a nation. I appreciate the slogan that our current president brought forth, but we cannot totally make "America Great Again" without God's intervention! I cry every time I hear the song, America the Beautiful. She's not beautiful anymore. She must return to God and His ways in order for that to happen.

We must plead to God for mercy and ask that we be granted repentance for the onslaught of the multiple abominations being hurled at such a Holy God on a regular basis! We must with reverence for God believe that the Church as well as America can still be *great and beautiful if she is granted such divine repentance!* Unfortunately it won't be without severe consequences for our sins and the chastisements, some of which have not been withheld and *more are coming*. Corporate judgments, chastisements and consequences are necessary for cleansing and spiritual awakening, but oh God "in wrath (anger) remember Mercy". (*Habakkuk 3:2*) SELAH

If this is too hard to hear and you are thinking about putting this book down, please don't. Your future and the future of your children may depend upon the truth that is exposed in this book. There are people that need to hear the truth that only you will be able to share with them. The truth is necessary in order to be able to plead our case before the Father.

Getting back to our example in the Old Testament of a nation in crisis much like ours, please note that God did give them a way out of their continual suffering but it was refused. (*Jeremiah 6*) Because of this, they were unable to retrieve their blessings and were doomed to more suffering as the *consequences* for their sins. The prophet brings his lament before God in the following passages of Scripture.

Please note: This didn't stop Jeremiah from praying through to the finish and we must continue also!

Jeremiah 8:18

"Behold the voice of the cry of the daughter of my people because of them that dwell in a far country. (*Those in bondage*) Is not the LORD in Zion? Is not her King in her? Why have they provoked me to anger with their graven images and with strange vanities? The harvest is past, the summer is ended, and we are not saved. For the hurt of the daughter of my people, I am black. Astonishment hath taken hold on me. Is there no Balm in Gilead; is there no Physician there? Why then is not the health of the daughter of my people recovered?"

Jeremiah is greatly disturbed about their condition because he is such a faithful prophet! He knows and is intimately acquainted with His God and connected to His purpose for them. These people belong to God and He knows that God promised them a great future, much like us. Why won't they hear Lord? You promised them healing and prosperity! What is wrong with them? What has happened to your people God?

Jeremiah continues his intercession:

Jeremiah 9:1 – 6

"Oh, that my head were waters, and my eyes a fountain of tears, that I might weep day and night for the slain of the daughter of my people! O that I had in the desert a wayfarers' lodging place; That I might leave my people, and go from them! For all of them are adulterers, an assembly of treacherous men. And like their bow they have bent their tongues for lies. They are not valiant for the truth on the earth. For they proceed from evil to evil. And they do not know me says the Lord. Everyone take heed to his neighbor, and do not trust any brother; for every brother will utterly supplant; And every neighbor will walk with slanderers.

Everyone will deceive his neighbor, and will not speak the truth; they have taught their tongues to speak lies; they weary themselves to commit iniquity. Your dwelling place is in the midst of deceit; through deceit they refuse to know me says the Lord."

There's the problem. This is why they aren't healed Jeremiah. This is why calamity has come and has persisted! It was the choices they made. They don't care about anybody but themselves! They have chosen to live in *self deception* and *denial*. To say that they were backslidden sounds kind of soft at this point. A stronger way to describe their condition would be to say that they were in full blown *apostasy* and only a remnant of God's people truly remained faithful.

These were some very serious sins against God! He was not at this point going to pretend that everything was ok. It wasn't! God is a responsible *parent* and *Covenant Partner*. He is bound to His laws of sowing and reaping even though He is the only One who could sign an Executive Order to the contrary, and only if He sees fit! They may be choosing to live in *deception*, but there's no deception in God. He knows His people and He knows what they need. Jeremiah had to tell them the truth about themselves even though he was persecuted for it. None of this was God's fault. His ways are perfect. He was not going to put a Band-Aid on their festering wounds.

Repentance from the heart and Spiritual cleansing had to come in order to preserve at least a *Remnant* of His people; those who would obey and follow Him! So, here comes the verdict.

Jeremiah 9:6
"Therefore, says the Lord of Hosts: Behold, I will *refine* them and try them; for how shall I deal with the daughter of my people? Their tongue is an arrow shot out; it speaks with deceit; one speaks peaceably to his neighbor with his mouth, but in his heart he lies in wait. Shall I not punish them for these things say the Lord? Shall I not avenge myself on such as nation as this?"

Refine - *Heb. Tsaraph* - smelt, refine and test; metaphor - bringing them through the fire and refining them as silver and trying them as gold is tried through the fire.

God let them know that He's going to allow the *hardships* to be used as this *fire/punishment* for the sins of the nation in order to purify as many as He can and turn them back to Him. This puts more grief into the heart of Jeremiah, but he knows God still loves his people. He realized that more prayer is needed for the people of God to be able to *endure* what is coming. Hopefully they would turn from their wicked ways and enjoy a glorious celebration!

Endure - *Webster's* - to remain firm under suffering or misfortune without yielding (*in this case, to continue to walk with God no matter what consequences they would face*).

In the following passage of Scripture we get a glimpse of one of the *secrets* of breaking through in prayer - *weeping, lamentation* and *travail* which we will cover later on.

Jeremiah 9:10 - 16
"For the mountains I will take up a *weeping* and a *wailing*, and for the dwelling places of the wilderness a *lamentation*, because they are burned up, so that no one can pass through; nor can men hear the voice of the cattle. Both the birds of the heaven and the beast have fled; they are gone. I will make Jerusalem a heap of ruins, a den of jackals. I will make the cities of Judah desolate, without an inhabitant. Who is the wise man who may understand this? And who is he to whom the mouth of the Lord has spoken, that he may declare it? Why does the land perish and burn up like a wilderness, so that no one can pass through? And the Lord said, 'Because they have forsaken my law which I set before them, and have not obeyed my voice, nor walked according to it, but they have walked according to the dictates of their own hearts and after the Baals, which their fathers taught them to do,' therefore thus says the Lord of Hosts, the God of Israel; 'Behold, I will feed this people, with wormwood and give them water of gall to drink; I will scatter them also among the Entities which neither they nor their fathers have known; and I will send a sword after them until I have consumed them.'"

In this passage of Scripture "*wormwood*" is a type of punishment for un-confessed sin. They were not repentant. They didn't even realize they were walking around in the *consequential chastisements* of the Word of God for what they had sown. Even their children were suffering for the sins of their parents! (*Jeremiah 9:21* and *Jeremiah 15:7*)

There are serious ramifications for breaking spiritual laws whether we know about them or not. That is why in His love and mercy He sends Prophets to warn His children because of the serious conflict they are about to face. When their cup of sin is filled and they have continuously ignored Him, the *spoken word judges them!* This is why Jeremiah was wailing and in deep lamentation.

The following Scripture helps us see the reasoning behind this principle.

Genesis 6:3

"And the Lord said, My Spirit shall not always strive with man, for that he also is flesh"

Strive - *Heb. Diyn* - to rule;

Strive - *Webster's* - to make effort.

God doesn't force His principles upon us; He only offers them to us as a way to health and prosperity. So what this says is that God will not *always* make an effort to change man's mind about sin. He's given him a free will and allows him the freedom to exercise it. If he sows to the flesh, he'll reap corruption. If he sows to the spirit, he'll reap God's kind of life in Christ. (*Gal. 6:7 & 8*) That settles it!

At this point Jeremiah had enough God-consciousness to know that God's laws were in motion and things were serious. There are also a few prophets in this nation that know this as truth and aren't afraid to speak it out, but unfortunately, are being falsely labeled as doom and gloom preachers. To tell you the truth, God did not change His laws of sowing and reaping; we have, in our foolishness, in order to govern ourselves! Therefore, we're in big trouble! Because the people were taking no heed to the warnings of this prophet, and like Moses and Abraham who preceded him and interceded for their nation and families during those "crisis" times, he quickly organized a prayer meeting and even called for the *"mourning (cunning) women"*!

Jeremiah 9:17
"Consider and call for the mourning (*wailing & lamentation*) women, that they may come; and send for the wailing women, that they may come! And let them make haste and take up a wailing for us, that our eyes may shed tears, and our eyelids flow with water" (*in repentance*).

He's saying, "Put the women to work!" This is serious! Gather all of them and let them come and be broken for the sins of the people and perhaps God will shorten the time of punishment. Weeping and true repentance is always music to God's ears much like when our children finally learn to listen to us!

In Joel's day even the Priests had to come out from the shadows and do *public displays* of weeping and repentance in their crisis situations.

Joel 2:17
"Let the priests, the ministers of the Lord, *weep* between the porch and the altar, and let them say, Spare thy people, O LORD, and give not thine heritage to reproach, that the Heathen should rule over them: wherefore should they say among the people, Where is their God?"

The important thing to remember is that both men and women of God are being called by the Holy Spirit to pray for their families and the future of this nation with a *prophetic urgency* and *fervency* like I've never seen before; the issue is that important. I strongly believe the reason why we are in such bad condition in this late hour is because we have not prayed like we should have. Our lack of prayer has revealed how far away we've strayed from God. He sets it as a *priority!* When we should have been united and strong as a corporate body of believers, we were not and because of it, we have become weak, powerless and ineffective. It's time to get up and do what God wants us to do in this hour!

Before we move on, I want us to remember that in regards to the *chastisements/judgments/punishments* God never deals with His people *vindictively*, but always with *redemption* in mind.

Vindictive - *Webster's* - disposed to seek revenge; intended to cause anguish or hurt

Redemption - *Webster's* - to buy back; to get or win back

The following is an article written by our overseer's wife (Jean Hodges) in response to a Vision and Word given for the United States in 1999. I've included it to show the reality of God warning His people and the redemptive cry of his heart through these people to pray for *mercy*.

Sounding the Trumpet
A call to Prayer
By: Jean Hodges

After waiting on the Lord and after praying, I saw a map of the United States. In the middle of the nation I saw what looked like a cesspool of quicksand. I was aware that cities were being pulled into it toward destruction, being devoured and going under. I cried to the Lord asking for the prophets to be sent to warn and the evangelists to cry out for souls.

The first city I saw being pulled into this quicksand was New York. Then other major cities on the rim of the quicksand came into my view; Chicago, Seattle, Los Angeles, Phoenix, Dallas and Miami. I began to ask the Lord to bring forth intercessors to rise up and bear His burden. As I waited on the Lord, I asked Him the meaning of the cities. He spoke to my heart that they represent the sins of our nation.

- **New York:** idolatry, worship of mammon with its heart In Wall Street
- **Chicago:** intellectualism and roots in humanism
- **Seattle:** self-sufficiency, disregard of God
- **Los Angeles:** love of pleasure and entertainment more than lovers of God
- **Phoenix:** sorcery, witchcraft and rebellion
- **Dallas:** self-righteousness, pride and religious spirit
- **Miami:** moral filth & decline, perversion, abortion, & Drug abuse

As I waited and cried out to the Lord to quicken me to pray, I saw a man standing in the middle of quicksand who

Luke 19:41 – 44

"Now as He drew near, He saw the city (Jerusalem) and wept over it, saying "if you had known, even you, especially in this your day (time) the things that make for your peace! But now they are hidden from your eyes. For days will come upon you when your enemies will build an embankment around you, surround you and close you in on every side, and level you, and your children within you, to the ground; and they will not leave within you one stone upon one another, because you did not know the *time* of your *visitation*."

Two things I want us to notice:

The Importance of *Timing* – God works in times and seasons

The Purpose of *Visitation* – He manifests (*comes out of the shadows*) reveals His divine plans either to warn or to bring blessings

Definitions:

Time – Gr. *Kairos* – refer to a fixed and definite time; the time when things are brought to *crisis*

Visitation - Gr. *Episcope* – investigation, inspection, visitation for the purpose of relief for their crisis and distresses

Revelation – Gr. *Apocalypsis* – Laying bare; a disclosure of truth or instruction concerning things unknown; manifestation; appearance

God works and accomplishes His purposes in *seasons* and *times*. Therefore, timing is a key element in getting those things accomplished by His people who can hear His voice. The following are Scriptures that prove this point.

Ecclesiastes 1:1
To everything there is a *season*, a *time* for every purpose under heaven

Ecclesiastes 1:15
He makes all things beautiful in His *time* (*eth* – Heb. - due season)

Isaiah 33:6
And He will be the stability of your *times*, (*eth* – Heb. - due season) A wealth of salvation, wisdom and knowledge; the fear of the LORD is His treasure.

Without receiving a full understanding of this truth, we would be left out of the picture and wouldn't be able to fulfill our destiny and purpose in God. We would miss opportunities to work with Him in finishing the work He started. We are not left on our own to do *our* will, but to do *His!* So we really must develop some discernment about our *times* and *seasons*.

Another passage that really helps us understand this is found in the Book of Chronicles as we talk about the tribe known as the Sons of Issachar. *Issachar* means - He is my reward or He is my wages. There are things we need to recognize and do in order to reap the *benefits* or *rewards* for knowing the timing of the Lord.

1 Chronicles 12:32
'And the children of Issachar which were men that had understanding of the times, to know what Israel ought to do,

the heads of them were two hundred and all their brethren were at their commandment.'

As I began to study about these guys, I realized that they were able to help Israel during a time of *national shaking* and *transition*. Saul and his sons were in a fierce battle with David and his men and they were sorely defeated. It was customary in those times that the losing King would fall on his sword and die. The cost to David was severe as he cried out in his grief of losing Jonathan, his best friend and son of Saul, "How the mighty have fallen in the midst of battle! Jonathan was slain in your high places". (*2 Samuel 1:25*)

Times of Shaking and Transition can really hold rough days ahead particularly if we don't understand what God is doing. Even when we do have understanding, there's a price to pay to follow God.

It was now time for David to organize his armies and reign as Israel's King as was prophesied. This was a very unstable time in Israel's history, but God was leading His people in the transition by people who *could hear His voice and understand the timing of the Lord!*

Right now we are going through some very *unstable times* of *shaking* and *transition* in our nation as well as the church. God is using many voices to help those who cannot hear Him; unfortunately many still refuse to listen. God is visiting His people and has been warning us through dreams and other prophetic means, that we have reached a critical stage of the crisis in our nation and something has to be done quickly. There is literally a crisis in every arena in the U.S. and it appears that it gets worse by the day.

In the late 90's He gave me a dream that greatly disturbed me about more *shakings* that we would have to endure. As I pursued God for the interpretation, I received great clarity.

My Shaking Dream

Job 33:15 - 18
In a dream, in a vision of the night when deep sleep falleth upon men in, in slumbering upon the bed; then he openeth the ears of men and sealeth their instruction that he may draw man (away) from his (own) purpose and hide pride from man.
He keepeth back his soul from the pit and his life from perishing by the sword.

I dreamed I was in my house having a large dinner party or celebration. There were windows all around us in the living room. I could see for miles and miles through those windows. As I looked closely, I began to see storm clouds brewing on the horizon; and on the North side of my house I saw the biggest, most formidable tornado I've ever seen in my life heading straight for us. I don't exactly know how wide it was, but it was huge and covered the entire sky! As it got closer, I began to shout and warn everyone in the house to follow us down to the basement but they were walking around like they hadn't heard a word I said. My husband and I were prepared and went downstairs as we begged others to come with us, but to no avail. We began to hear the howling sounds that tornadoes make and the house began to *shake*. It sounded like a freight train was headed our way as it got louder and louder; and it seemed like only a few seconds later it was right in our front yard. The house shook so hard that I could feel my teeth rattling in my mouth! I woke up frightened, expecting to see all of my teeth in the bed or on the floor! That's how vivid it was. I was shaken in my spirit and very much concerned!

I knew through experiencing God's voice in dreams before that something really bad was coming. I was even afraid to ask the Lord what it was, but when I did inquire of Him, He told me that our nation was going to experience a series of *shaking(s)* and that we were going to pass through several very serious *fires!*

I really didn't know what to do with this bit of information, so I just shared it with my husband and our overseer's wife, Jean Hodges in Dallas. That's when I learned of the vision I shared in the previous chapter "Sounding the Trumpet". I knew I wasn't crazy! I called my friend Marilyn in Mississippi, who is an intercessor and she said she was feeling the same way. She didn't quite know what it was, but it wasn't good. Neither one of us had any idea of the magnitude of the *shakings* that would occur on September 11th, nor the fires of racism being stirred up again, the killing of police officers at random, massive storms and floods and fires, the immigration crisis, and at present the rebellion against the laws of our land, as well as lies and propaganda being fed to us by many media outlets, etc. on a daily basis. Phew!

Several weeks before the tragedy in New York one of my friends in Mississippi, who is also an intercessor, shared how he was unable to sleep well at night and knew we were headed for more shaking that would strike like a "woman experiencing labor pains". We were greatly disturbed in our hearts and asked God for mercy.

As I sought the Lord and searched the Scriptures for

confirmation, He led me to the book of Haggai. The findings are as follows:

Haggai 2:6 – 9 & 21-22

"For thus says the Lord of hosts, 'Once more in a little while, I am going to *shake* the heavens and the earth, the sea also and the dry land. And I will shake all the nations; and they will come with the wealth of all nations; and I will fill this house with glory.' says the Lord of hosts. 'The silver is Mine and the gold is Mine', declares the Lord of Hosts. 'The latter glory of this house will be greater than the former,' says the Lord of hosts, 'and in this place I shall give peace,' declares the Lord of Hosts.' "Speak to Zerubbabel governor of Judah saying, 'I am going to shake the heavens and the earth. And I will overthrow the thrones of kingdoms and destroy the power of the kingdoms of the nations; and I will overthrow the chariots and their riders, and the horses and their riders will go down, everyone by the sword of another. 'On that day,' declares the Lord of hosts, 'I will take you, Zerubbabel, son of Shealtiel, my servant,' declares the Lord, 'and I will make you like a signet ring, for I have chosen you,'" declares the Lord of hosts.

Even though these passages were written for those times, God was showing me that *shakings* were sometimes necessary and that there would be many *shakings* in many generations including an imminent *shaking* coming to our nation, with more to follow in the days ahead. He assured me that I wasn't to fear, but to trust Him. I began to warn others to turn back to Him, as I shared with them what God had shown me.

Definitions:

Shake - *Heb. Undulate* - to make waves

Shake - Gr. Seio - To rock (*vibrate, sideways to and fro*) i.e. to agitate (in any direction; cause to tremble; to throw into a tremor (*of fear or concern*); to move, quake and shake.)

"Shaking" - Wilson's Bible Dictionary of Types and Shadows, is a symbol of "the removal of all things that do not have their foundation in Jesus Christ".

Wow. This all made sense to me even though I wasn't happy about it. I continued to pray for wisdom and revelation.

Very soon after that time, as I shared with you in the previous chapter, my husband and I transitioned to OK from Kansas. After being there for a little while I received an invitation to speak at a church in a city nearby where we were. They asked if I could speak for three meetings, Friday night, Saturday morning and Saturday night. I was very excited especially since I didn't know any of these people. As I prepared, the Lord told me to minister on "*The Shaking*"! I thought I was really going to get a chance to make an impression on these guys, right? NO! I begged God to let me speak on something else but He won in the end.

As I came forward to speak on the first night, people were still coming in and some were even coming in off the highway on foot because they had heard a meeting was going on. The place was packed! I opened the book of Haggai and read the aforementioned Scriptures, after which I was led to share My Shaking Dream. The place was so quiet that we could have heard a pin drop on the carpet! I then began to teach about the symbolism and meanings of words etc. and how a shaking could apply to us today. Everyone was listening so intently. I later found out they had never heard of a *prophetic dream*, (another *secret* to breaking through in prayer) or anything *prophetic* at all. They were just hungry and wanted to learn more about the Holy Spirit! It turned out to be an awesome night in God! I had to share what I meant by using the word *prophetic* and gave them a Scriptural reference to help them understand more clearly.

Prophetic - *Gr. Prophetikos* - words spoken by someone anointed to speak something for God (usually a prophet; spokesman). In other words, something spoken by God through a man or woman anointed of the Holy Spirit.

<u>Numbers 12:6</u>
"Then he (God) said, Hear now my word: If there is a prophet among you, I the Lord, make Myself known to him in a vision; I speak to him in a dream"

The next morning, much to my surprise, the place was packed again, but the really unusual thing was that there were no pastors. They decided not to show up. I thought it was odd but their excuses seemed really legitimate. They were young and had small children so I figured we were alright. I'm trying to get to the part where people do not want to listen to the voice of the Holy Spirit, especially when it's about the timing of the Lord and crisis! It's unfortunate, but they never showed up for the morning session or the night time session either; we had powerful meetings in spite of it and no one seemed to be unsettled! I shared with the people that during times of *shaking*, God uses it as discipline and helps us get rid of our "sins and weights that so easily beset us" and how He would help us re-evaluate our priorities to be able to better walk with Him. Our team prayed with those precious people for almost two hours after each session. The Saturday night meeting even brought in a miracle provision from a man (a stranger to the congregation) who was driving by on the highway. He said the Lord spoke to him to come inside and give (the lady speaker) an offering – and afterwards he left! I was pretty impressed with my God for speaking to someone on the highway to help us with our expenses and provide such a "more than adequate" offering!

God had come out from the shadows, just like He did for Abraham under the oaks of Mamre (*a place of vision/seeing*) in <u>Genesis 18</u> and ministered to all of us powerfully even though the message was tough! Those who had ears to hear heard what the Holy Spirit said to them and they were better prepared to face whatever the *shaking* would eventually bring.

I'm sure many of you may be curious about what happened with those precious leaders. It's not a good report, but I'll summarize: the pastor didn't believe in the Holy Spirit and later told my husband and I that we'd probably do better by moving up the road to a larger city if we wanted to preach about Him; his wife, though Spirit filled was conflicted with her husband's views and eventually left him and remarried someone else and moved away. I'm just glad I didn't know about anything because God had a purpose for us being there. A few months later, the first *shaking* known as 911 happened! Those precious people who heard the warnings were prepared and even though the shaking was very severe, they knew God was with them and would see them through it. Many of them got in touch with our ministry and thanked us for the *clarity* it brought.

Shakings cause us to wake up. I hope it's clear that I am not saying God causes these shakings; *permit's* them as consequential judgments/chastisements would be a better way to describe them. This last episode in New York and at the Pentagon (911) is *part* of that shaking that I saw in my dream. That shaking woke me up in the middle of the night and since then, I've heard so many people say that this tragedy was a *"wake up call"* to America. I remember when I was in high school and my alarm clock would go off. I would simply press the snooze button and eventually it would go off again, and in a few minutes . . . it would go off again . . . and then in a few minutes, it would go off again until my mom would come in the room and insist that I get up. In fact, she wouldn't leave my room until I got up. People of God, it's that *time.* Only, it's not my mom standing in the door, its Jesus. And He's not going to leave us until we "get up" and do what we're supposed to be doing!

I honestly believe we've arrived at our *Kairos* time; remember, it's a *strategic* time; a set or proper time; an *appointed* time; a *most opportune* time; a *due season.* Yes, we've been brought to *crisis* because of our sins. People are calling good, evil and evil good. Sin is tolerated even in many churches because we don't want to correct or offend anyone. The Holy Spirit isn't allowed to move freely in His power because man wants control and is afraid it would offend their congregations! That's not the right way to think about God! He doesn't care a bit about political correctness much less be told He cannot move in a service because He might offend someone! Something really bad has happened to us as Christians when this happens and we need to wake up and deal with it. Thank God He hasn't given up on us.

I found something very interesting in one of my books I received in Bible School, Crisis Counseling. I read that the Chinese have a symbol for the word *crisis*; on one side it says *crisis* and the other side *opportunity*. God was speaking and I was listening. I believe He has given us a window of opportunity to get something done that should have already been done. The Scriptures tells us to *"redeem the time"* for the days are evil. (*Ephesians 5:16*) In other words, we are to "buy back" those opportunities we missed while we were sleeping". We must recognize that by God's grace, we've been given another *opportunity* to get our house (*the church*) in order. We must also be reminded that He's given us *power* for these *times* that could make positive changes in the future of our nation for generations to come.

Luke 10:19
"Behold, I give unto you *power* to tread on serpents and scorpions, and over all the power of the enemy and nothing shall by any means hurt you."

Power – Gr. *Exousia* - the ability or strength with which one is endued, which he either possesses or exercises. Authority, jurisdiction, liberty, privilege, power, right, strength; delegated authority and influence

A Church that has been caught off guard by the enemy isn't going to be effective in prayer when crisis hits if she has no *power*. A church that has fallen asleep will not be prepared to meet the challenges of a nation in spiritual and moral decline without this *power*. We must access and use this *power*; first of all, in consistent and effective prayer for all people; in preaching and teaching a sound gospel of Jesus Christ, and in living our lives as *authentic witnesses* as we demonstrate God's love and mercy with extraordinary signs, wonders, and miracles following us! His power is here to heal, restore and deliver us.

Isaiah 57:18
"I have seen his ways and I will heal him; I will also lead him, and restore comforts to him and to his mourners."

I believe if we hear His voice and obey His commands we will get to participate in perhaps one of the greatest outpourings of His Spirit that neither you nor I have ever seen before.   I believe with all my heart that God wants to heal America of its wounds, and use the church to usher it in.

Jeremiah 30:17
"For I will restore you to health and I will heal you of your wounds, declares the Lord."

I'll say it again. Timing is everything! The time is now. It's time for us to awaken from our sleep and redeem (*buy back*) the time that we have lost! How do we do that?

Four

Come up Higher!

As I was looking back and thinking about the night I was awakened by the Lord with an urgency to go to prayer, I remembered something very important He showed me about His Servant Abraham. When He began to speak to him about the "latter issue", (*judgment to Sodom and Gomorrah*), he told him exactly what He was thinking about doing, but not how it would affect His family. It was like God knew it would provoke Abraham to pray for them. It's just like the Scripture says, "God always knows what our needs are, but He wants us to pray"! (<u>*Matthew 6:8*</u>) The problem I have with all of that is why can't more of us hear and obey? I myself have struggled with this very same thing more times than I want to admit.

One weekend as I began to seek Him and pray for the right message for a conference I was hosting in Oklahoma City, I asked Him that question. He said *one* of the main reasons was because His people don't come up high enough to hear Him clearly, which then causes them to be easily distracted with life, and at that point, they are more prone to become *complacent*. Ouch!

Complacent - *Heb. Sha-anan* - at ease; false sense of security; at ease; careless; arrogant

He continued the thought by saying that He has been calling the church to come up higher for a long time, but she was comfortable where she was. That was a very sobering word to hear from Him. It saddened me to think that we could so easily refuse a request from Him. It touched me so deeply that I became aware that He was speaking to me too! I began to realize how selfish I had become with my life. I cried out to Him and repented. I knew I had felt empty inside for months, but continued avoiding some very pressing issues. I was really running on empty for about six months after receiving a bad medical report about our Phoebe, my precious little mild-mannered but mischievous weenie dog of 12 years! Losing her was not on my list of things to prepare for. I was so overwhelmed by these circumstances that I could hardly bring myself to prayer. At least I received my theme for the Conference – Come up Higher!

As I began searching the Scriptures for developing my message for the theme "Come up Higher", He led me to the Book of Songs in Chapter 2 and showed me His desire for His church through this beautiful allegory. This is rather lengthy but we'll get through it quickly and explain what He's saying to us.

Allegory – *Webster's* - A story, poem, or picture that can be interpreted to reveal a hidden meaning, (*secret*) typically a moral or political one; a symbol

<u>Song of Songs 2:1- 10</u>
"I am the rose of Sharon and the lily of the valleys. As the lily among thorns, so is my love among the daughters. As the apple tree among the trees of the wood so is my beloved among the sons. I sat down under His shadow with great delight, and His fruit was sweet to my taste."

He brought me to the banqueting house, and his banner over me was love. Stay with me flagons; comfort me with apples; for I am sick for love. His left hand is under my head and His right hand doth embrace me. I charge you Oh daughters of Jerusalem, by the roes and by the hinds of the field that ye stir not up nor awake my love until He pleases.

The voice of my beloved; behold he cometh leaping upon the mountains, skipping upon the hills. My beloved is like a Roe or a young hart; behold he stands behind our wall; he looks forth at the windows, showing himself through the lattice; my beloved spoke, and said unto me "Rise up my love, my fair one and come away.

For lo, the winter is past, the rain is over and gone; The flowers appear on the earth; the time of the singing of birds is come, and the voice of the turtle is heard in our land; the fig tree puts forth her green figs, and the vines with the tender grape give a good smell. Arise, my love, my fair one, and come away.

O my dove, that are in the clefts of the rock, in the secret places of the stairs, let me see they countenance, let me hear thy voice; for sweet is thy voice and thy countenance is comely. Take us the foxes, the little foxes that spoil the vines; for our vines have tender grapes.

I told you it was lengthy. Here, if you can see this, is a picture of Jesus calling His bride to come to the *high places* with Him. She is sitting in the shade of His presence, enjoying the blessings of belonging to him, etc. and He appears to come out of the shadows to call her out of her *"comfort zone"*, as I see it. He speaks so sweetly to her and allows her to continue basking a little longer. After all, His banner over her is love. She then pleads with Him "don't take the flask of wine away or the fruit I'm eating; you know it's my favorite Lord. (*I'm paraphrasing of course*) I could sit here forever"!

Knowing her very well, He has to remind her that the season has changed; the winter is past; the springtime has come and it's time to prune the vines; and oh by the way, you might need a change of clothes and some boots for you must come up higher and follow ME to the mountains!

The book of Habakkuk refers us to those places in the following verse:

<u>Habakkuk 3:19</u>
"The LORD God is my strength, and he will make my feet like hinds' feet, and he will make me to walk upon mine *high places*."

High Places - *Heb. bama* - to be higher; higher ground; high place of worship; high place of battle; high on the mountain; connotation of a place of *wisdom* and *insight*; vantage point, to be placed above your enemies.

Reference to "mine high places" - This makes what Habakkuk is saying more personal: it is a more suitable place, one that fits each one of us individually; my own place in God; not only in good times or season of God's blessings, but when it appears that nothing good is happening.

High Places in the Scriptures also refer to the following:

1) An exalted place
2) An elevated place
3) A place of power
4) A place of honor

5)   A place of unusual knowledge
6)   A place of heightened perception

Notice in particular the last two: Knowledge and Heightened perception.

Perceive – *Webster's* – to notice or become aware of something;   keen sense of discernment;

Discernment – *Webster's* - the ability to see and understand people; things, or situations clearly and intelligently

I remember certain times in my life that I needed clarity so badly. There were a lot of voices speaking into my life at that time and I was very distracted. I couldn't tell which one was the voice of the Lord and which ones were the voices of men. I even had prophets speaking to me; the sad part of that deal was that they were all saying different things! I needed to hear and see clearly. I had to get away from the voices of man and come up higher to hear the voice of the Lord. God then spoke to my heart that I would have to get into my cave, so to speak, and learn to *cultivate* a hearing ear and a seeing eye. That's when I found this promise.

Proverbs 20:12
The Hearing Ear and the Seeing Eye, the Lord has made them both

Definitions:

Cultivate – *Webster's* – try to acquire or develop; to foster the growth of something; break up the soil in preparation for sowing or planting.

Hearing - *Heb. Shama* - hearing with a renewed interest; listen with the intent to obey.

Seeing - *Heb. Ra ah* - to see; to look at, perceive beyond natural ability; to discern; distinguish

This was so powerful to hear. We must understand our own *prophetic times* and *seasons* (another *secret to breaking through in prayer*) and how important it is to hear what God is saying to us. We must recognize that we must take personal responsibility to cultivate the ground of our hearts in the *high places* of God's presence.

In this allegory God was calling her to those high places so she could hear and see! She would be able to discern the signs of the times and the things that were ahead of her. She would also recognize that she needed to get rid of things in her life that had "snuck in unaware" during her season of *complacency*; things that if left unchecked would disqualify her from being able to complete her race with joy. One commentary said, "In the high places she is able to discern that there are things that could potentially ruin her walk with Jesus, make her dull of hearing and maybe even *disqualify* her from participating in His plan for the harvest in her future.

The Bible calls them "foxes".

Vs. 15
"Catch for us the foxes, the foxes that are spoiling the vine"

Foxes represent the crafty, cunning and wicked ways of men which include false teaching and false prophesying;

preaching and merchandising God's people for filthy lucre to satisfy their lust and greed for the things of this world and have no interest in the things of God. These foxes seduce men and withhold the pure word of God from them for fear they will lose control of them and the money they bring! The book of Jude identifies them as falling into the "error of Balaam" (*preaching for their own profit*) and those who are walking in the ways of "Cain" which one Commentator stated as (*murdering the innocent souls of men with falsehood*).

The Apostle Paul confronted these foxes in his day and told us they were perverting the gospel which would create great loss. (*2 Cor. 11*)

God wants us to hear with a *renewed interest* all the things He wants to say to us during these troubled times. Previous generations have failed to hear the urgent call to arms in prayer and have suffered great losses because they were distracted with so many things. That does not have to be us! We must recognize our "*kairos*" times and adjust accordingly to do the will of the Father. Remember, God's ways are different from ours.

Through my association with a brother within our ministerial family, I found four (4) valuable strategies that I have continued to develop over time that can really help us to come up higher and respond to God's urgent call to intercessory prayer. (*Thank you bro. Eric Reeder*)

Strategy – *Webster's* – a careful plan or method to afford the maximum support in achieving success

Important Strategies:

1. *Elevate for Illumination*

    Elevate – *Webster's* – to lift something up; to make higher; to raise a standard or in today's vernacular "to raise the bar" "step up my game" etc.

    In other words, we all need improvement and need to come up and spend some time with God and become pro-active in learning to cultivate our *spiritual* ears. We cannot afford to bypass this very important strategy.

    <u>I Cor. 2:14</u>
    "But the natural man does not receive the things of the Spirit of God, for they are foolishness to him; nor can he know them, because they are spiritually discerned."

    Discern – *Gr. anakrino* - to be able to examine or judge for understanding

    Our minds must be renewed if we are to be able to truly follow God.
    <u>Romans 12:1 - 2</u>
    "I beseech you therefore brethren, by the mercies of God, that ye present your bodies a living sacrifice, holy, acceptable unto God, which is your reasonable service.
    And be not conformed to this world: but be ye transformed by the renewing of your mind, that ye may prove what is that good, and acceptable, and that perfect will of God."

    We must develop a new way of thinking in order to understand *spiritual things* like *timing* and *changes of seasons*. We must learn to follow the leading of the Holy Spirit in prayer as Jesus taught and not pray according to how our natural man/flesh sees things.

<u>*Isaiah11:1 – 4*</u>
"And there shall come forth a rod out of the stem Jesse, and a Branch shall grow out of his roots. And the Spirit of the Lord shall rest upon him, the Spirit of wisdom and understanding, the spirit of counsel and might, the spirit of knowledge and of the Spirit of the Lord. And shall make of quick understanding in the fear of the Lord: and He shall not Judge after the sight of his eyes, neither reprove after the hearing of his ears; But with righteousness. . ."

2. *Evaluate Your Life*

Evaluate – *Webster's* – to determine the significance, worth or condition; careful appraisal and study.

It's time for self examination when you get to this point. No excuses. You're in preparation and must be willing to follow through to the end. Look at your situation; but observe with great clarity.

Clarity – *Webster's* – The quality of being clear; the quality of transparency or purity; the quality of coherence and intelligibility; the quality of being certain or definite about something.

This sure sounds like a lot of work! Yes it is but I promise it will be well worth it when you find yourself in the presence of God, responding to His call. You will remember who you are and who you belong to. You will discover pertinent information about your life and your calling.

2 Cor. 13:5

"Examine yourselves, whether you are in the faith; prove your own selves. Know ye not your own selves, how that Jesus Christ is in you, except ye be reprobates."

I know this is strong, but we are no longer to live to please ourselves, but to please Him who lives in us.

3. *Eliminate the Hindrances*

Eliminate – *Webster's* – remove; get rid of

Hindrances – *Webster's* – things that provide resistance, delay, or obstruction to something or someone; hinder – to make slow or difficult the progress; to hold back

Many things hinder our spiritual progress.

- No Fresh Revelation
- Religion and Traditions of Men
- False & Erroneous Teaching
- Fear of Man
- Disobedient Heart
- Spiritual Laziness
- Bitterness
- Selfish Motives
- Rebellion
- Escapist Mentality

If we don't have understanding of how important prayer is, we won't accomplish God's will in our times. Since prayer (*communication with God*) is the primary way the Lord get's His will accomplished, we cannot afford to tolerate ignorance in that department.

Tolerate - *Webster's* - to allow things (bad, unpleasant or harmful) to exist without doing something about it.

Hebrews 12:1 - 3
"Wherefore seeing we also are compassed about with so great a cloud of witnesses, let us lay aside every weight, and the sin which doth so easily beset us and let us run with patience the race that is set before us, Looking unto Jesus the author and finisher of our faith; who for the joy that was set before him endured the cross, despising the shame, and is set down at the right hand of the throne of God."

Removing things that hinder us is a form of cleansing; but there is an even deeper cleansing we must all go through to come up higher and be productive in the work of prayer.

2nd Cor. 7:1
"Having therefore these promises, let us cleanse ourselves from all filthiness of the flesh and spirit, perfecting holiness in the fear of God."

Cleanse - Gr. *Katharezo* - to make clean; like a *catheter* being used to force uncleanness out so our bladders won't burst.

I know this is a strange way to say it but remember, we're comparing it to spiritual cleansing. Also, please notice in that verse that there are two things being targeted for cleansing.

Physical Sense – from outward stains and dirt

Moral Sense – from inward sins – motivations and faults; purify from wickedness; To free from   guilt   of sin; then to consecrate and dedicate ourselves to the Lord

1 John 2:16
"For all that is in the world, the lust of the flesh, the lust of the eyes, and the pride of life, is not of the Father, but is of the world."

4. *Engage in Prayer*

Engage – *Webster's* – to enter into contest or battle with an enemy

Matthew 11:12
"And from the days of John the Baptist until now the kingdom of heaven suffers violence and the violent take it by force"

We must contend for those promises in the Word of God only from a *cleansed* position! Un-confessed sin weakens us!

Contend – *Webster's* – assert something as a position in an argument; struggle to surmount (a difficulty or danger); engage in a completion in order to WIN.

Let's remember what happened to Joshua's men when they went out to defeat the city of Ai in _Joshua 7_.

God told them to go take the land of Ai; so they sent spies and saw that "the people of Ai were few" and decided the land could easily be taken without exhausting all of their men; in other words this was easy pickings! (Joshua 7:3) What they didn't know was that there was sin in the camp that would be exposed when they went to fight that would cause them to all run away in fear and lose the battle; suffering a loss of thirty-six (36) men. Shocked, Joshua cried out to the Lord and He (the Lord) did not mince words. "Get up; Israel has sinned; my judgment fell; now "sanctify the people!" (A _Secret to Breakthrough_) Chapter Eight shows them once again engaged but this time they defeated their enemies!

We must remember that our fight is in prayer; but we fight from a _cleansed position_ if we are going to experience victories!

The aforementioned passages show us the hard truth. Sin causes us to be unable to stand before _God_; unable to stand before _man_ and unable to stand before our _enemies_!

The Bible teaches us the how-to's for us to become those warriors who know how to get the job done through prayer. It is definitely time to engage in prayer!

The benefits for engaging in prayer:

1. Brings us into the right kind of relationship with the Father.

2. Gives us power against the works of darkness

3. Releases the workings of God in the earth

Five

The Secret Place

Now, I truly believe that deep down inside our hearts we have a desire to pray for others. That's not the problem. I believe our lack of prayer for others is not only due to ignorance or not being able to hear God's voice, but we haven't yet learned to pray effectively for ourselves. We sort of treat prayer as a last resort when things get really bad and then it becomes crying and begging God to do something, many times in unbelief!

Matthew 6:6
"When you pray, (not if) , go into your inner room, and when you have shut the door, pray to your Father who is in *secret*, and your Father who sees in *secret* will repay you."

Secret – Gr. *Kryptos* – hidden, concealed

God tells us here that prayer is a *necessity* to life that will bring great benefits and rewards, but we have to seek Him from our *inner man* or the *hidden place* in our heart.

The secret place (A *secret to breakthrough in prayer*) represents a place of solitude or being alone with God. It also represents a place where there are no distractions.

It's a place where we learn to hear the voice of God and learn to discern or fully recognize God's presence. Great men and women of God found this *secret place*.

Moses found his secret place in a *"little pup tent in the wilderness where God would meet with him."* (*Exodus 33:7 - 11*)

It is written that the presence of God was so strong that all of Israel would bow in silence when Moses was visiting with His God in that place. That was some secret place!

Elijah found his secret place when he learned how to seek after God with all of his heart. He discovered that he had to get past all the hype of religion, traditions of men, and the hustle and bustle of everyday life in order for him to hear the *"still small voice"*. (*1ˢᵗ Kings 19*)

Ruth discovered her secret place when she lay at Boaz's feet all night, until he took notice of her. (*Ruth 3:9*) It was then she made her request known to him.

David of course, cannot be forgotten! He found out that his "secret place" was dwelling in the shadow of God's wings. (*Psalms 91*) This was where David received his encouragement, instruction, and strength to go on. The collection of Psalms we enjoy today came out of his personal experiences in the secret place.

All of these great men and women of God knew how to find the *secret place*. And because of it they were able to enjoy:

- Great Revelations of God
- Great Relationship with God
- Great Experiences in the Glory of God

Because of pressing into their secret place they became *spokesmen and intercessors* and were able to give birth to God's purposes for their generation.

The call to the church as we've seen in the previous chapter has always been to come to the "*secret place*".

<u>Song of Songs</u> 2:14
"O my dove, in the clefts of the rock, in the "secret place" of the steep pathway, let me see your form; let me hear your voice; for your voice is sweet and your form is lovely."

This is God speaking *intimately* to His church. This is saying, 'come be alone with me, be like my servant Moses". It was said of him that the Lord spoke "face to face" as a man speaks to a friend. (*Exodus 32:11*) Moses was a personal, intimate friend of God and vice versa.

Intimacy - *Webster's* - close or warm friendship, in our case covenant; a feeling of belonging together, close familiarity or association

God desires *intimacy* (*close or warm friendship*) with his servants. In his book, <u>Chosen to be God's Prophet,</u> Henry Blackaby makes this profound statement that changed my life: "A lost world depends on the vital relationship of the people of God with their God. To lose this closeness with God (*intimacy*) is to lose our significance in the world."

Vital - *Webster's* - Necessary to sustain life

If we don't find that *Secret Place* with Him, we will be unable to pray and see things turned around and lives transformed.

<u>Daniel 11:32</u>
". . . but the people who *know* their God shall be strong and carry out great exploits".

The word *"know"* implies being in personal relationship with God; first hand information about God; being His personal friend; being able to enjoy close friendship with Him. Spending intimate time with Him purifies us for the work He's called us to and puts grace in our hearts to do it.

<u>*Proverbs 22:11*</u>
"He who loves purity of heart, and has grace on his lips; the king shall be his friend."

God and Moses had an awesome relationship that greatly inspires me. <u>*Psalms 103:7*</u> says that God "made known His ways to Moses". Moses didn't just know *about* God, he knew God. He spent time in the *secret place* with Him. He got away from the people and the hustle and bustle of life and climbed the mountains to be alone with his God.

It was said of Elijah that "he was a man just like us" yet when he prayed....the results were a little bit more different than ours! (*James 5*) His prayers rocked heaven. He had such a relationship with God that even the weather could be altered when he prayed as commanded.

He could be bold about what he was saying because he had spent time finding the *secret place* and having those private meetings with God. (*This is definitely another key to breakthrough!*)

The Apostle James encourages us to walk so closely with God like Elijah did, that our faith would be strong enough to heal people!

What is it that hinders so many of us from finding this "secret place"? Does each of us have our own "secret place"? I want to submit to you three (3) fears I believe we face when we begin to seek the Lord concerning these matters.

1. Fear of the Unknown

2. Fear of Encountering Ourselves

3. Fear of Standing Silent before Almighty God

#1 - Fear of the unknown

First of all, we've never been this way before. We've never walked in the Spirit before we came to Christ. And many of us still don't! We're used to walking after our own ways, following our own plans instead of Gods; but God does not make it easy for us to find the "secret place" either. He likes to challenge us! He told the bride in Song of Songs to climb up the mountains into the "cleft of the rocks" and the "steep pathway". If you've ever gone mountain climbing you'll understand more clearly that this is not talking about going on a picnic! This is pressing . . . like the apostle Paul stated in _Philippians 3:14_ - "I press towards the mark for the prize of the high calling of God in Christ Jesus."

Press - Gr. _Dioko_ - Pursue aggressively; run swiftly against all odds; using force against resistance. It takes effort and tenacity to pursue an audience with Him in certain seasons of our lives. Why? He's issuing a challenge to us that He knows will eventually make us _stronger_.

Everyone who wants to go further with God and find their *secret place* will have to go to what the Bible refers to as "the wilderness". There they will find the following:

1. Testing and trials

2. Humbling

3. Self Discovery

<u>*Deut. 8:2 - 6*</u>
"And you shall remember all the way which the Lord your God has led you in the wilderness these forty years, that He might humble you, testing you, to know what was in your heart, whether you would keep His commandments or not. And He humbled you and let you be hungry and fed you with manna which you did not know, nor did your fathers know, that He might make you understand that 'man does not live by bread alone', but man lives by everything that proceeds out of the mouth of the Lord."

I believe what He says in vs. 15 of that same chapter strikes *"fear of the unknown"* in us. He calls the wilderness, *"great and terrible"* and says there are *"fiery serpents and scorpions"* there. Oh joy! I can't wait to go there. But these simply represent temptations, possible attacks of the enemy and days of having to totally depend upon God. These things will be used for our training and cleansing and help us learn to put our trust in God instead of ourselves. It's a place where we get our eyes opened!

Isaiah 42:16
"I will bring the blind by a way they did not know, I will
lead them in paths they have not known. I will make
darkness light before them, and crooked places straight.
These things I will do for them."

Even though the wilderness seems like a "scary"
place, it is still a good place. Let's overcome the fear of
the unknown. The Bible says that if we draw back in
fear, God takes no pleasure in us. He reminds us that
"The just shall live by faith." (*Hebrews 10:38*) God's
loving-kindness is going to meet us there and carry us
through; but we must allow Him to take us there.

#2 - Fear of Encountering Ourselves

I don't know about you, but I've realized that all the
inner conflicts I go through are usually with me! I try
to run from her, but everywhere I go she shows up! In
the wilderness we will learn that most of our battles in
life are not with others but with ourselves. Being alone
with God will always involve conflict with our "flesh
man". We might as well get ready!

In *Romans 8,* Paul tells us that the mind of the flesh is
in "enmity" with God and cannot please Him. Enmity
is intense hatred. Our flesh (*natural*) man hates our
spiritual man. That's why Paul said he had to "buffet
his body". Buffet is the word that means "rap with the
fist" "to beat down". This involves inner conflict.

Conflict - *Webster's Dictionary* - War; a clash between
hostile or opposing elements, ideas, or forces

We don't like to admit it, but when we spend time with God we will have conflict with ourselves and conflict with God until our spirit man comes into agreement with His will.

When Jacob spent the entire night alone with God, there was great conflict. God was trying to do something "in" Jacob so He could do something "for" and "through" Jacob. Many of us are trying to fight and resist the devil, when in many cases, we are fighting against God. It's our flesh waging war against His Spirit!

The following are clues or warning signals that we are running from ourselves and in essence, running from God.

1. We always want to have people around. This keeps us from facing ourselves and the real issues that separate us from God. We turn on the T.V. for company instead of going into the secret place. It's non-conflicting unless you're like me and want to yell at the TV for all the foolishness going on in the nation, especially in the political arena.

2. We settle for unhealthy relationships with friends; even that's better than confronting ourselves.

3. We spend hours at the mall . . . searching, searching, searching, trying to fill that inner void with something other than what we already know is there for us.

4. In the secret place we'll discover things we don't like about ourselves; secret sins; bad habits; attitudes that need adjusting. Believe me, we won't want to admit them much less make adjustments!

5. While we're alone, we will struggle with lies and accusations of the enemy; condemnation, thoughts from our past; rejection from family, regrets, etc. This will sometimes involve issues that cause us great pain as we face them once and for all. Then we will have to learn how to pray against spiritual wickedness in high places, tear down strongholds in our minds, etc. You know, *Ephesians 6*!

All of this is very challenging but if we don't face the truth, we cannot continue victoriously with God. Our hearts will be too weighed down with stuff! We'll continue to walk in what the Bible calls "self deception".

Jeremiah 17:9
"The heart is *deceitful* above all things, and desperately wicked; who can know it? I the Lord search the heart, and test the mind; Even to give a man according to his ways, according to the fruit of his doings".

Deceitful – *Heb. "aw kobe"*. That which is fraudulent - crooked, deceitful, and polluted; in other words, it needs cleansing. Being alone in the "secret place" will produce that cleansing.

We also see this truth in David's prayer in his secret place when he prayed.

Psalms 139:23 - 24
"Search me Oh God, and know my heart; Try me and know my anxious thoughts; and see if there is any *hurtful* way in me, and lead me in the everlasting way."

Hurtful - NAS – *Heb.* crooked - "contrary to God; perverted."

Many times we are in stressful situations caused by those hurtful, perverted ways in us, but through prayer, *we* can be straightened out before we try to straighten everybody else.

Hebrews 12:12
"All discipline for the moment seems not to be joyful, but sorrowful; yet to those who have been trained by it, afterwards it yields the peaceful fruit of righteousness. Therefore, strengthen the hands that are weak and the knees that are feeble, and make straight paths for your feet, so that the limb which is lame may not be put out of joint, but rather be healed."

In other words, the writer of Hebrews is telling us not to stay *crippled*. We are to admit that there are things wrong with us and go to God so He can heal us.

#3 - Fear of Standing in Silence before God

Zecharia 2:13
"Be still before the Lord...because He has aroused Himself from His holy dwelling. . ."

Zephaniah 1:7
"Be silent before the Sovereign Lord...."

Many times we cannot hear from God because we simply won't be quiet. I'll share this story with you.

A Very Talkative Evangelist

I remember attending a meeting in Glenwood Springs, CO with my friend Gwen. There was a young Evangelist preaching that night and he really had a good message. At the end of his preaching time, he felt the Lord instructed the congregation "to be silent before Him". There was a gentle hush that fell over the place and the presence of God came in but unfortunately didn't get to stay very long. There were people crying, some falling on their knees and worshiping softly underneath their breath, while others were basking in that Holy Presence. I just knew that God wanted to move in that place and do something special in the lives of His people. Unfortunately, this was cut short. The Evangelist never really stopped talking; only paused shortly after he'd say something! He didn't heed his own instruction and what seemed to be about a total of two (2) minutes of silence, he abruptly started his sales pitch to purchase his teaching materials at the back of the sanctuary. It was as if someone threw a wet blanket on the entire congregation. I knew instantly that we had _grieved_ the Holy Spirit! It was at that time I had a vision. I saw an arm extended to us that looked like a prosthetic arm with a hook on the end of it. I asked God what this meant. I thought He might

have wanted to heal someone or do a creative miracle and grow out an arm had we been silent. But God interrupted my thoughts and I heard Him say so clearly "that was a very lame attempt by man to be silent in My Presence". Instead of seeing the arm of the Lord, we saw the lame arm of man.
SELAH

Why is *silence* such a threat to us? Why do we find it so hard to be quiet in His presence? Let's dig deeper. I believe silence becomes unpleasant for us because of one or more of the following reasons:

- In silence we will have to listen to our inner man in whatever condition he/she is in. We may be whimpering and in pain from the past. We may be so angry that we want to keep it buried because we could "blow" a fuse at any given moment and hurt people. We may have to face the fact that we're not really saved; a fraud. In silence before God, our cover is blown. Everything is brought to the light. In silence, we feel the pangs of guilt for failures and past mistakes that keep haunting us and bringing condemnation.
- Condemnation robs us of faith to stand in the Holy Place; therefore we keep running from Him.
- In silence we may hear the "still small voice of God" and not want to admit some things about ourselves and our situations. God may ask us to do something we are not willing to do. (*Forgive people who had hurt me in the past was one of my big struggles.*)
- In silence we face our fear of the future, fear of dying and most of all an unhealthy fear of our God!

- Silence can be very threatening if we don't know ourselves.
- Silence before a Holy God makes us *vulnerable*.

What does it mean to be vulnerable?

Vulnerable – *Webster's* - capable of being wounded; susceptible to wounds; open to attack or Scrutiny

To be vulnerable is part of the curse of the fall. After Adam and Eve sinned (*something they had never experienced before*) they decided to take things into their own hands. They tried to cover themselves with fig leaves, something the glory had done for them before they sinned.

The same thing happens to us. Our vulnerability causes us to run away from God instead of to Him. We become like Jonathan's son, Mephibosheth, who "fell and became lame" and "fled" from King David. (*2nd Samuel 4:4*). After a few years King David sent his men out to see if there was anyone in Jonathan's house that he could bless and bring to the King's Table. This is a type of the love of God that never gives up on seeking us but finds us hiding out in fear and shame. Many times we run and hide from God because we don't want to face Him like we are. (*Mephibosheth had lame feet*) We know we're crippled but we don't know how much He loves us and wants us healed. Many hide in religion, traditions of men or behind wealth and social status; while there are others who grow up in poverty and feel as if they are doomed in this life to live as eternal victims of society because of never having the opportunity to do otherwise. The urban dictionary calls this group of people "social casualties". This is such a lie!

Listen, we're not fooling God. We must come out from behind the shadows and our "false coverings" that hide the real truth about our *desperate need for Him*. We must embrace the truth that we can come out and come to Him just as we are! He knows the secrets of our hearts. When we allow ourselves to get closer to Him on occasion, we know that He knows them! That's what we run from!

The "secret place" is where we strip off the old and put on the new. I believe God is tired of us "faking it until we make it"! God is not going to be mocked. Either we have Him and serve Him, or we don't. He's not indebted to prove Himself to man if man is not going to seek after Him sincerely, and with his whole heart. Yes, in His mercy He will drag us sometimes to the *wilderness* but the process is rough; He begins by removing our props!

The Psalmist said, "Before I was afflicted, I went astray, but now I keep your Word". (*Psalms 119:67*) That's why we have a wilderness . . . we get to know our own hearts.

In the Book of Hosea, God speaks of His intentions in bringing Gomer, the unfaithful wife of His prophet Hosea to the *wilderness*. I want you to notice that God doesn't bring this sinful, adulterous woman into to the wilderness to beat her down or condemn her. Listen to what He says:

Hosea 2:14
"Therefore, behold, I will allure her, bring her into the wilderness, and speak comfort to her. I will give her vineyards from there, and the valley of Achor as a door of hope; she shall sing there, as in the days of her youth, as in the day when she came up from the land of Egypt. And it shall be in that day, says the Lord that you will call me 'my

Husband' and no longer call me 'my Master', for I will take from her mouth the names of the Baals and they shall be remembered by their name no more."

In the wilderness, we are purified by God's holy love.

Psalms 103:8 – 9
"The Lord is compassionate and gracious, slow to anger and abounding in loving-kindness, He will not always strive with us, nor will He keep His anger forever."

As long as we are willing to repent, God will remove all those things that we hide behind and all those things that we worshipped in His place. We enter into what the writer of the book of Hebrews call "the rest of God." Then He joins us wholeheartedly to Himself and we become one with Him.

(1st Cor. 6:17)
"He that is joined to the Lord is one with Him."

Joined – Gr. *Kollao* - "to glue, to glue together, cement, fasten together; to join oneself to; to cleave

In our wilderness experiences we learn to cleave to no one else but Jesus and our lives are transformed. The writer of the book of Songs observed the bride coming up from her wilderness experience and said "Who is this coming up from the wilderness, *leaning* on her beloved". (Song of Songs 8:5)

Leaning – Heb. *raphaq* - to recline; rest in Him

In other words, she quit striving. She quit leaning on props. She quit trying to be someone she's not. The great pretense is over. She can say like Jacob, "I have seen God face to face, yet my life has been preserved"! (*Gen. 32:30)* Now she can pursue the call of God on her life and even learn to pray for others at strategic times of His choosing!

Let's make it one of our priorities to find our own secret place and pursue God. Let's run "to Him" and not "from Him". He has great rewards that we will never know anything about if we run from that appointment.

Six

The Cries of the Righteous

I hope you've recovered some valuable truths from the previous chapters and are ready to proceed in discovering some things you may not have known or perhaps put aside for lack of understanding or more revelation. I believe we're at the place in the church and the nation where we have no other recourse but to face the truth. We can no longer walk in deception. We are in need of repentance on a corporate level in our nation and a whole hearted return to God and His ways in our homes and our churches. It's the only antidote for our spiritual condition and you could possibly be the *intercessor* that helps make it happen!

Antidote – *Webster's* - A remedy to counteract the effects of poison; something that relieves, prevents, or counteracts

We can get a glimpse of the power of an *antidote* when we read about the Israelites being led through the wilderness by Moses. They came to the waters of Marah and couldn't drink the water.

Exodus 15:22
"So Moses brought Israel from the Red Sea and they went out into the wilderness of Shur and they went three days in the wilderness and found no water. And when they came to Marah, they could not drink of the waters of Marah, for they were bitter: therefore the name of it was called Marah (*bitter*). And the people murmured against Moses, saying 'what shall we drink?' And he cried unto the Lord, and the lord showed him a tree, which when he had cast into the waters, the waters were made sweet."

In this passage, one commentator writes, "we see the children of Israel's great escape from the clutches of Pharaoh, the Miracle at the Red Sea, and the great supercharged celebration that followed! When they reach the Waters of Marah or bitter waters as they are referred to in the text, we get to see something else: a tired, emotionally drained, fearful bunch of people who have arrived in unfamiliar territory called the wilderness"; not a palace or nice hotel to get a good hot bath and some good food and later venture out and find a Starbucks for a good cup of coffee. (*I added that of course*) NO! Their deliverance had only begun – it was a frightening-looking wilderness and they were faced with water they couldn't even drink! That's when the grumbling and complaining started.

Moses knew how bad things really were, and although he was just as tired and thirsty himself, he immediately cried out to the Lord for their answers. (*Thank God for leaders, including moms and dads who really know what they should do in crisis situations!*)

After I read this account over and over, not really knowing what I was looking for, I came to an astounding truth about this man Moses! He was eighty (80) years old – not a young and feisty state of the art preacher of today with the latest technology, bags of money and/or fancy buildings and cars, – but an eighty-year old man on foot! Excuse me; I had an epiphany. (*A moment of sudden revelation or insight*) I was strongly encouraged that it's never an issue of age, social status or financial success for preachers, male or female, moms or dads, to become great *intercessors* to deliver their own children or collectively God's people through their prayers and intercessions. Alright, we can move forward.

Exodus 15:25
"Then he cried out to the LORD, and the LORD showed him a tree; and he threw it into the waters, and the waters became sweet. There He made for them a statute and regulation, and there He tested them."

This is where we see a demonstration of what a *righteous intercessor* is all about. Moses responded immediately to the needs of the people. We need them today as we face the battles ahead in the cleansing and reformation for sure. He knew he had to reach God for these people in order to receive the right instructions. God gave them what they needed and they moved forward in the will of God; and God will speak to you as a parent also to show you what's necessary for the saving of your household, whether you are single or married. Don't doubt it! Leaders, Business owners; He will do the same for you.

I know a lot of books have been written on intercessors and intercession and I do not claim to be an expert on the subject, but I have learned that once you've prepared yourself, you must *"just do it"*. There's been much talk about prayer and plenty of seminars and conferences have been held in honor of prayer but let's get real. There have been very few people willing to get understanding and pay the price in prayer! We need to quit talking about it and go to God for answers. To quote E.M. Bounds, "To pray is the greatest thing we can do; and to do it well there must be *calmness, time* and *deliberation*".

Did you notice those three (3) words "Calmness, Time, and Deliberation"?

Calmness - Implies reconciling ourselves to the matter; not losing our composure or position in prayer; not praying in unbridled fear, but rather learning to pray in faith as we are led by the Holy Spirit.

Time - Implies recognizing we must be patient and focused as we continue in prayer, fully trusting that that God makes "all things beautiful" in His time.

Deliberation - Implies long and careful consideration; slow and careful movement as we proceed in intercessory prayer.

I want us to note that these three (3) things are what the flesh (our carnal nature) absolutely hates! Yes, we dread it sometimes and it's going to be a battle to follow the leading of the Holy Spirit and not the leading of our natural man. I just thought I'd throw that in there in case you thought it would be easy.

The Bible's definition for intercessor is as follows:

Intercessor - *Heb. paga* - to impinge; to stand between; cause to entreat; to cause to meet together

My Definition - "one who goes to God on behalf of someone else or does someone else's praying for them".

In the above story we see an entire nation of God's holy people being prayed for by one *righteous intercessor;* Moses. God needs men and women to pray for "all men" including those who *do* know God and are in need of strategic prayers against the attacks of the enemy, and those who *don't* know God, for them to have an encounter or appointment with the Father.   The Scriptures   prove   this   to   be   true.

Intercession for people and situations bring *encounters, answers, antidotes* and wards off *enemy attacks*. Look out now!

You're more powerful in prayer than you know. In this passage for example, God gave Moses an *antidote* for the bitter waters.

As Israel's intercessor, he received instructions to throw a "tree" into the waters so the waters would be made sweet.

Sweet – *Heb. Mathaq* – to be or become sweet or pleasing; to suck; to give a sweet taste

I love this. Long before the children of Israel knew about the cross that Jesus would carry for their sins and the crucifixion that would take place, we can get a glimpse of this by what Moses was told to do in order to purify the water. Even though I've heard several messages saying that this was a word of knowledge with a scientific slant given to Moses about the type of tree to use to purify the waters, I knew there was a deeper meaning and significance to this instruction. The tree was a foreshadowing of Jesus Christ and how He sweetens the bitter things in our lives and turn our sorrows and suffering into blessings. (Wilson's Bible Dictionary of Types and Shadows)

It then occurred to me that the Book of Ruth had the same scenario going on with Ruth's mother-in-law, Naomi, whose name meant *pleasantness* but wanted to change her name to Mara (*bitterness*) after she lost her husband and two (2) sons prematurely. Because Ruth followed her and took care of her return back to her people, Naomi was restored to her purpose when Ruth married Boaz, a type of our Savior Jesus Christ. Naomi was not only saddened and embittered because she lost her husband and two sons, but also her posterity; but God was so gracious to Naomi through her daughter-in-law and gave her grandchildren to nurse and tend. Thank you God for the Old Testament writings to encourage us and point us to the Savior and His goodness! Naomi's waters were made sweet again and she lived out her later years with love, grace and dignity.

Hebrews 4:15

"He is a faithful High Priest who is touched by the feeling of our infirmities."

Infirmities – Gr. *Asthenia* – feebleness (of body or mind) by implication; malady; moral frailty: - disease, infirmity, sickness, weakness.

Ignorance, Sickness, and **Moral weaknesses** could also be considered infirmities that the savior helps us to overcome. (*More on this later*)

Because Jesus can be touched or sympathizes with our weaknesses, He is able to help us if we cry out to Him, even on behalf of others. I tell people that "we are a sign that God has indeed made a Covenant with man" and he permits us to participate in gathering in a harvest of souls in each generation through our prayers. It's in our hands!

Prayers from *righteous* men and women who are in *Christ* are able to prepare men's hearts to receive the word of God because they are anointed and led by the Spirit of God to pray effectively for them. The prayers of *righteous* men and women hold the keys to suffering humanity!

James 5:13 - 16
"Is anyone among you suffering? Let him pray. Is anyone cheerful? Let him sing psalms. Is anyone among you sick? Let him call for the elders (spiritual leaders) of the church, and let them pray over him, anointing him with oil in the name of the Lord. And the prayer of faith will save the sick, and the Lord will raise him up. And if he has committed sins, he will be forgiven. Confess your trespasses to one another, and pray for one another, that ye may be healed. The effective, fervent prayer of a righteous man avails much."

I realize this passage of Scripture is talking about getting people in church healed, but the principle I'm looking for is there. Fervent, earnest, consistent, heartfelt prayer from *righteous* people who are in Christ, coupled with confession of our sinful condition is what brings the healing hand of God. Powerful things happen when the righteous men and women of God begin to pray!

Psalms 34:15
"The *eyes* of the Lord are upon the righteous and His ears are open to their cries."

Righteous people are very important to God obviously! In Christ, we're the link between God and man. Seeing Moses demonstrate the power of God simply because he was righteous really interested me and I realized God was preparing me for truth that would extend God's mercy and grace to a church and a nation in crisis.

I want to bring forth an example in Scripture that shows how important it is to maintain our righteousness before God especially when representing God to the people and the people to God; in other words, the priesthood which in today's language is known as the leadership. If you are weak or fainthearted this will be very hard to hear.

As I began my search to hear what He wanted me to hear about this I stumbled on Eli, a Priest in the Old Testament and his not-so-righteous sons who served the priests in the Tabernacle. They were continuously sinning and breaking the Holy Laws of God. Eli was warned at least two (2) times by the Lord that I know of; [1] by an unnamed prophet and [2] by the child, Samuel who at that time was being groomed to be "God's Prophet". They told him to deal with his sons or face severe punishment. Basically, he was being told to "restrain them or remove them". He did neither and it was said that because he honored his sons more than he honored the Lord, great tragedy fell upon the house of Eli and they all died prematurely.

I want us to remember that when God deals with leadership it's because He has you on his mind! Another thing to remember is that the sometimes extreme disciplinarian action He permits didn't come without warning! God always warns before He chastises!

In *1 Samuel Chapter 4*, Eli gets the news that his two sons died in a battle with the Philistines and the ark of God was stolen. When Eli hears this, he falls off of his stool, breaks his neck and dies also. Meanwhile, while his daughter-in-law was giving birth to a son, she gets the news and cries out "Ichabod", meaning *"the glory has departed"* and she also died! *This was a rough day in Shiloh for sure! SELAH*

I knew instantly what God was saying to me. Since Eli's story was one of an unfaithful priesthood who had dishonored and greatly offended a Holy God by failing to rebuke or reprove sin, especially in its leadership, I could see through much of my travels and experiences as Evangelist/Teacher that many of the churches were heading in the same direction! Please go online and purchase my book, <u>The Scent of Water</u>: Hope and Healing for Relationships. In it, I share about the brokenness and loss many church people were enduring needlessly, due to the hidden *sins* in the leadership. The following is one of those stories.

A Distraught Pastor's Wife

This woman called me at 5:00 in the morning, after three (3) days of preaching every night in their church; needless to say, I was exhausted. In fact, after I agreed to meet with her, on my way to the car, I didn't notice the cactus garden I was parked next to, and fell flat on my face in it! Thank God there wasn't a scratch on me; but I did question whether or not I should be driving anywhere that morning in my condition! I could only say afterwards that I was glad I did.

She called me in secret because she not only wanted to be discreet but was afraid her pastor husband would find out about our meeting. She told me that she believed her husband was having an affair with the church secretary. He was coming home late at night and had been lying to her about his whereabouts. She said she tried talking to him but to no avail. He would yell and scream at her and would get so angry he began to physically push her around. I could see in her countenance that she was visibly afraid of him and in need of a word of wisdom from the Holy Spirit for assurance that she would do the right thing.

After being told she was crazy and overly suspicious for several months, she weighed the option of going to the church leadership (*those who sat in positions of authority*). She trusted them to give her sound advice. Unfortunately they didn't believe the accusations she made against her husband. Instead they told her the same thing her husband told her. They accused her of being overly suspicious. They honestly felt that he would never do anything to jeopardize his reputation or the reputation of the church. Their advice to her was that maybe she was just overworked and needed a vacation.

Once her husband found out that she had gone to the leadership and told them her suspicions, he grew more and more verbally abusive to her and the children. She was so afraid of him losing control and hurting them that she decided to ask me what to do. I told her to pray for courage and grace and confront him again. I also told her to bring someone with her that would protect her should he get physical. We ended our meeting with prayer as I offered her hope for the confrontation. After several weeks had passed I received a call from this woman relaying the events that had unfolded since our meeting. She finally had convinced one of the church leaders to approach her husband with her in a non-threatening place; his own office. When confronted, her husband lost his temper and became very violent, throwing things around, yelling and screaming at his wife.

His violent and defensive reaction prompted a meeting of the board of directors. They decided that the Pastor should take a sabbatical (vacation) with pay for a couple of months to seek counseling and take care of his problems with his wife and children.

To make a long story short, he did not heed the determination of the Board nor did he return home. Instead he cleared all of the money out of the bank account of that church, took the new car they had given him earlier that year, and left town with the church secretary he had been seeing for six (6) months. Several months later the couple divorced and he married the other woman and started another church!

In the *Book of Ecclesiastes*, which is a book traditionally attributed to Solomon, and consist largely of reflecting on the vanities of human life, I found a passage that could apply directly to points I am making concerning hidden sins in leadership.

Ecclesiastes 10:1
Dead flies cause the ointment of the apothecary to send forth a stinking savor; so doth a little folly him that is in reputation for wisdom and honor.

Although in many cases I was able to share valuable insight to help people deal with the *sins* that were committed against them, it was only after the damage had been done and many would suffer for a long time. I could tell you horror stories, but the Lord won't let me. It was very shocking and disheartening to witness. I knew we were heading for more trouble and open shame because we were not honoring God in much the same way as Eli and his sons.

Ministers/Leaders have an obligation to not only tell people the *truth* about sin and its consequences but to also walk above reproach themselves. This doesn't mean that they will never make mistakes, but must be ready to pay a high price. God takes these things very seriously. Fear of man will not be tolerated as well as rebellion, witchcraft or any other kinds of sins as far as God is concerned. Ministers will give answer to God for the things they teach, preach and live! The Apostle James even warns those who aspire to *become teachers* to be aware of the fact that they will be held to a *higher standard* and a stricter *judgment.* (*James 3:1*)

It was during this season and time that I began to see great ministers and their ministries fall. It was a rough time in Christendom! It was very heartbreaking to watch and definitely brought humility to my life. I remembered the Scripture in *1 Cor. 10:12* – "Therefore, let him who thinks he stands, take heed lest he fall."

Why was God so hard on Eli's house I thought? How does that apply to us? One commentator wrote that it was because the priesthood was unable to lead the people of God in the right way because they themselves weren't walking in it (*which by the way, God takes very serious*) and had lost their effectiveness to those around them; the same being true today. The following is a quote by Henry Blackaby in his book <u>Chosen to be God's Prophet</u> that I've mentioned before, but bears repeating.

"A lost world depends on the *vital* relationship of the people of God with their God. To lose this closeness with God is to lose our *significance/effectiveness* in the world."

The following definitions clarify how serious this is.

Definitions:

Vital – *Webster's* – necessary to sustain life

Significance- *Webster's* - The quality of being worthy or important

Effectiveness - *Webster's* - the degree to which something is successful in producing a desired result; success

Pretty eye opening isn't it? "To whom much is given much is required." (*Luke 12:48*)

Jeremiah, Isaiah, Ezekiel and others lamented over horrific conditions in the people of God during their watch also.

Jeremiah 23:11
For both prophet and priest are profane; yea in my house have I found their wickedness, sayeth the Lord.

Isaiah 28:7
But they also have erred through wine, and through strong drink are out of the way; the priest and the prophet have erred through strong drink, they are swallowed up of wine, they are out of the way through strong drink; they err in vision, they stumble in judgment.

Ezekiel 22:28
And her prophets have daubed them with untempered mortar, seeing vanity, and divining lies unto them, saying Thus sayeth the Lord, when the LORD hath not spoken!

Unless and until we take this *gift of righteousness* more seriously than we do at present, things are not going to turn around. The church has been given an opportunity to ask for the "*old paths, where is the good way, and walk therein.*" (*Jeremiah 6:16*) as previously discussed; hopefully she won't respond like the children of Israel did in that day by saying "We will not walk in them."

Seven
Awake Oh Sleeper

It is very important for all of us to remember *not* to take our righteous status with God for granted. It's a free gift but even though it comes with ambassadorial privileges, there are also important responsibilities that must be taken care of. While in Colby, KS in the late 90's I had the following dream that showed me this truth.

The President's Body Guard

I dreamed it was raining very hard and I was standing outside with a few people around me. An ambulance pulled up in front of us and the attendants walked up to me asking for me by name. Once I affirmed who I was, they opened the door of the ambulance and rolled out a gurney with an extremely overweight, dead man upon it. I was of course shocked at the sight. I asked who he was and what he died of. They told me he was the bodyguard of the President of the United States of America and that he had died of a massive heart attack. I was shocked and feared for the President's life. Something rose up in me in that dream and I jumped up on top of that dead man and started doing CPR and proclaimed "Rise and be healed in the name of Jesus!" The dead man immediately rose up, lifted his hands and began praising the Lord! The people standing around us started jumping up and down and throwing handkerchiefs in the air, rejoicing along with him. This caused crowds coming from all around us in a great celebration. I then received a call from the white house for a special job to do for the President.

After the dream, I sought out some people I trusted in the Lord and shared it with them. We all agreed with what God was saying. We were in danger and exposed to enemy attacks! The Body Guard (*the armor bearers; watchmen, gatekeepers, intercessors etc.*) all which represented the prayer ministry in some way, had died of fatness and laziness and had fallen asleep. It was the same universal problems the body of Christ faced at different points in history; usually rebuked for taking God's blessings for granted and forgetting to be salt and light for others. In other words, *complacency* had set it.

This dream marked a turning point in my life about the importance of being a *righteous intercessor* and what that really meant about our roles in prayer. From the very beginning of my walk with God, I knew my main focus would be prayer and intercession even though I didn't fully understand it. It was a revelation I will cherish for the rest of my life. God does not need a sleeping church who is *shirking* her responsibilities while reveling in the light.

Shirking – *Webster's* – avoid or neglect a responsibility; be unwilling to do something hard or difficult

Jesus said in <u>John 9:4</u> that he "must work the works of him that sent me, while it is still day: the night cometh, when no man can work." We have to remember that prayer is doing the "works of the one who sent us" or He would not have said "His house shall be called a House of Prayer for all Nations". (<u>2nd Chron. 7:12 – Matthew 21:13</u>) There's one more thing to note before we move on. Did you notice in the above Scripture reference in <u>John 9</u> that He said there was a day coming when our time would be up!?

Can it ever be too late to pray? I don't want to wait to find out. Let's just wake up and man our post.

Ephesians 5:14 – 16

Wherefore He saith, Awake thou that sleeps, and arise from the dead, and Christ shall give thee light. See then that ye walk circumspectly, not as fools, but as wise, redeeming the time, because the days are evil.

Definitions:

Awake – *Gr. Egeiro* – to arouse, cause to rise from sleep; to arouse   from the sleep of death.

Sleepest – *Gr. Katheudo* – to fall asleep; drop off to sleep; metaphor: to yield to slothfulness (lazy) and sin; to be indifferent to one's salvation.

Dead– *Gr. Nekros* - One that has breathed his last; deceased, departed; destitute of life – Metaphor: spiritually dead; destitute of a life that recognizes and is devoted to God because he's given up to laziness, trespasses and sins.

Wow. It's pays to look up what the words mean! We should read that again! We can have a better understanding when we realize the following truths about being asleep spiritually. I shared them in my Awakening Prayer Classes in both Oklahoma and Texas. Everyone was sober and pensive!

Truths about being asleep spiritually – the sleep of death

1. This exhortation is to *Christians, not unbelievers.*
2. We can be *asleep* and *not know* that we're asleep.

3. This is dangerous because we lose our *spiritual awareness* of what God is *saying* and *doing* and what the *devil* is *saying* and *doing!*
4. *Preachers* can still *preach* and *teach and be asleep!*
5. We still *look* like *Christians.*
6. We can sing our songs of celebration and hold great concerts etc. and still be spiritually dead.
7. We can even *think* while we're sleeping.
8. When we are asleep we *only* care about *ourselves.*
9. When we're asleep we *don't care* about *our neighbors.*
10. We don't care about *winning souls*, who goes to heaven or otherwise.
11. When we are asleep it is ok for us to be comfortable – that's enough – *it's all about us* being comfortable.

We must wake up! Falling asleep is the fruit of *Complacency.*

Complacent – *Heb. sha anan* – at ease, careless, arrogant; smug or uncritical satisfaction with oneself or one's achievement; no longer caring about what God cares about, etc.

Go back and read what the Lord answered in response to Jean's question concerning where the church was in her Vision and Word for the U.S. (Chapter Two).

Look at what Isaiah said to the women of His day. He wasn't mincing words either!

<u>*Isaiah 32:9 - 18*</u>
"Rise up, you women who are at ease and hear my voice; give ear to my word you complacent daughters; Within a year and a few days you will be troubled, Oh complacent

daughters; for the vintage is ended and the fruit gathering will not come. Tremble you women who are at ease; be troubled you complacent daughters; strip, undress and put sackcloth on your waist;

Because the palace has been abandoned, the populated city forsaken; Hill and Watch-tower have become caves forever, A delight for wild donkeys, a pasture for flocks; Beat your breasts for the pleasant fields, for the fruitful vine, for the land of my people in which thorns and briars shall come up; Yea, for all the joyful houses and for the jubilant city.

Until the Spirit is poured out upon us from on high, and the wilderness becomes a fertile field, and the fertile field is considered as a forest. Then justice will dwell in the wilderness and righteousness will abide in the fertile field and the work of righteousness will be peace and the service of righteousness quietness and confidence forever; then my people will live in a peaceful habitation and in secure dwellings and in undisturbed resting places;"

As I read this, I knew many of us were at that point and some of our situations were dire! After sharing my dream with our church, we all began to press in asking God to forgive us and awaken us to what His needs were as they pertained to praying for dire situations.

First of all there have been some pretty crucial Presidential elections since the turn of the century, and look at the intense battle going on today – it's not about personalities etc. but about policy that agrees with what God agrees with! You might want to re-visit the 4 sins I mentioned earlier that bring a nation down! We've got them all! This should show us the need for fervent, consistent, heartfelt prayer from righteous people for those who will lead our *civil government* or Paul would not have told Timothy to put it first!

At the time of the dream, I knew there were others praying and eventually the call would grow louder and louder! Intensity in prayer was very much needed at that time and the needs are still great today. There have been a few breakthroughs, but so much more is needed! The battle for the right kind of leadership is still as great as it was back then and now even more exposure is surfacing revealing man's motives, the hatred for those who support what God supports and the corruption that's been hidden for decades! I believe it's going to get extremely dirty as we go forward; sin will get bolder and hatred will be extreme; and the righteous have a really good fight on their hands!

I want to say here that after September 11, 2001 I truly believed in my heart that we would experience an *awakening* and that we as a people had recognized the importance of maintaining God's standards and would turn back to Him. Even though many of us would come to recognize our true spiritual condition and repent and return, I was sadly disappointed when many of the prophetic warnings continued to fall on deaf ears. For the following few months, the churches were filled to capacity with people wanting God but in order to truly be born again requires more than an emotional response to tragedy. SELAH I'm sure there was a remnant that stayed and searched long enough to find Him. Unfortunately, reports of church attendance began to drop and many churches even closed their doors. What happened? People went back to sinning and offending God? I'm not sure, but this only intensified the seriousness of the hour and the acute need for more prayer! Unfortunately, we as a nation continued our downward spiral along with our immorality and selfishness. It seemed as if 911 had never happened! Many were concerned but felt powerless to do anything about it.

The Scriptures tell us that "righteousness exalts a nation, but sin is a disgrace to any people." (Proverbs 14:34)

At that time, I felt that we as a nation had "forfeited the grace and favor of God" and "clung to our worthless idols" like the City of Nineveh in Jonah's day. (Jonah 2:8) God promises to protect a nation that is in right standing with Him. I mentioned earlier that I had heard one minister say that the tragedy in New York was because of "persecution for righteousness sake", but as a whole I knew our nation was not righteous. If it weren't for the prayers of the righteous we would have already been destroyed! We must remember that as Christians we are "ambassadors" defined as high ranking officials of the Kingdom of God and we hold the keys to the survival of this nation!

That is why Paul told Timothy to put prayer and intercessions as a priority as we saw in the very first chapter of this book! We have to remind ourselves that prayer is an on-going battle at strategic times whether it is for ourselves, our families or our country.

Matthew 11:12
"And from the days of John the Baptist until now the kingdom of heaven suffers violence and the violent take it by Force"!

Violence – *Gr. Biazo* – to use force; apply force

Does this mean we force people to believe like we believe? NO! What it means is to be *zealous* but have knowledge and wisdom in our preaching and teaching and live lives that reflect our message of love, grace and truth and continue to pray. It means we get our heads out of the sand concerning whether or not Christians should hold positions in the Civil Government because we are all getting ready to fly away any day! (*Sorry for the Sarcasm – not sorry*) We need to wake up! Of course they can hold offices and they should! That is all I'm going to say about that!

Prayer is one form of showing our love for all nations and people. Jesus said to pray this way: "Thy Kingdom come, Thy will be done on earth as it is in heaven" until we see it! Pray it until we see our families come to Jesus; pray it until we see our churches wake up; pray it until we see our nation truly become "one nation under God indivisible with liberty and justice for all".

The truth we have to face is that our crisis situation never really left since 911; more prayer and intercession is needed for breakthrough. Even though I believe there are many that have awakened since 911 and are even meeting in homes and businesses etc. for prayer, still more is needed! I truly believe in my heart that people today are slowly waking up and many will go through what I've called a "late awakening". Once awakened their zeal will ignite the fires of repentance and reformation in ways we never imagined!

The people who have a heart to "hear" will also have a "heart to work" until the job is done and this nation is turned around. Those who hear the voice of the Spirit will begin to follow as long as God's people are praying. This type of people realize there is something wrong with the spiritual foundation of our country and have an anointing to pull a remnant of people together to work to repair it. "God is not willing that any should perish, but that all would come to repentance." (*2 Peter 3:9*) It's going to take a lot of hard work, dedication and commitment to "pull it off" but through *prayer*, God's *greatest work* can be done.

Eight

A Lamb for a House

In this chapter we are going to discover another powerful *secret to breaking through* in prayer – applying the blood of Jesus.

Exodus 12:13 – 14

"And the blood shall be to you for a token upon the house where ye are and when I see the blood, I will pass over you, and the plaque shall not be upon you to destroy you, when I smite the land of Egypt. And this day shall be unto you for a memorial; and ye shall keep it a feast to the LORD throughout your generations; ye shall keep it a feast by an ordinance forever."

The Passover in the Old Testament Scriptures is the focal point of understanding the power of the blood. All sacrifice that proceeds after that in the Mosaic system is founded on this principle: through the blood of sacrifice, there is *deliverance, protection* and *hope* for our future. This mighty forecasting picture was fulfilled in the Person of Jesus, the Last Adam.

The following passage of Scripture gives us a little more insight to the plans and purposes of God through blood sacrifice. Solomon had just finished building the temple and prayed to God on behalf of the people he was to reign over.

2nd Chronicles 7:12 – 16

"And the Lord appeared to Solomon by night and said unto him, "I have heard thy prayer and have chosen this place to myself for an house of *sacrifice*. If I shut up the heavens so

that there is no rain, or if I command the locust to devour
the land, or if I send pestilence among
My people, and My people who are called by My name
humble themselves and pray, and seek My face and turn
from their wicked ways, then I will hear from heaven, will
forgive their sin, and will heal their land. Now My eyes shall
be open and My ears attentive to the prayer offered in this
place. For now I have chosen and consecrated this house
that My name may be there forever, and My eyes and My
heart will be there perpetually."

Sacrifice - *Heb. zebeck -* "a place of slaughter; that is the flesh
of an animal; by implication, a sacrifice of a victim; a place
of offering sacrifice".

Many times people searching for truth often ask me the
unanswerable question "why blood". I still don't fully
understand but I can offer up truth that needs to be
appropriated by faith, simply trusting that God's ways are
not ours. The following passage allows us a peek into truth
about blood.

Lev. 17:11
"For the life of the flesh is in the blood, and I have given it
to you on the altar to make atonement for your souls; for it
is the blood by reason of the life that makes atonement".

God could not draw near to His people without a
sacrifice being made for sin.   Blood had to be spilled and
offered to God as atonement for our sins. Because life is in
the blood, this was a type and shadow of what the spilling of
Jesus' blood would do for us. It would bring us back from
death into life.

Ephesians 2:1

"And you He made alive, who were dead in trespasses and sins, in which you once walked, according to the course of this world, according to the prince of the power of the air, the spirit who now works in the sons of disobedience, among whom also we all once conducted ourselves in the lust of the flesh, fulfilling the desires of the flesh and of the mind, and were by nature, children of wrath, just as the others. But God, who is rich in mercy because of His great love with which He loved us, even when we were dead in trespasses, made us alive together with Christ . . ."

Obviously this is not talking about physical death, although one day our bodies will die because of sin.

Romans 5:12

"Therefore, just as through one man sin entered into the world, and death through sin, and so death spread to all men, because all sinned. . ."

The death Paul is talking about here is spiritual death.

Romans 6:23

"For the wages of sin is death, but the free gift of God is eternal life in Christ Jesus our Lord".

Since life is found "in the blood" as *Lev. 17:11* tells us, Jesus' blood was the only thing that could bring us back to spiritual life in God! His blood was the atoning sacrifice that satisfied the wrath of God for the sins of mankind. *Romans 3:25* uses the word "propitiation" for Jesus' atoning sacrifice in His blood.

It means that Jesus became an "atoning victim" or a "scapegoat".

One of the Hebrew words for atonement is "Kaphar" which means "a primitive root, to cover; figuratively to expiate or condone, to placate or cancel: to appease, to cleanse, disannul, forgive, be merciful, pacify, pardon, purge away". Literally, in the fullest sense of the word, it means to clean us so good that it will be like we never sinned!

We see the first spilling of blood in the Garden when God killed an animal and used the skins to cover Adam and Eve. Since the Old Testament is a shadow of things to come, we can see that this was a type of the spilling of Jesus' blood to cover us and set us free from our sins. That "place of sacrifice" in Chronicles also represents the place where Jesus would die on the cross and be offered up to God as a "sweet smelling aroma". (*Ephesians 5:2*) So now God is able to draw near to us because of the blood of Jesus. We are reconciled back into fellowship with Him.

Ephesians 2:13
"But now in Christ Jesus, you who formerly were far off have been brought near by the blood of Christ."

The writer of the book of Leviticus makes another statement that brought me into a deeper revelation of the blood of Jesus.

Lev. 17:14
"For as for the life of all flesh, its blood is *identified* with its life". <u>NAS</u>

Identified-*Heb. Neh fesh*-a breathing creature - *Webster's* "to regard as identical; to associate; to establish the identity of".

The second definition is much better! Once we receive the blood sacrifice of Jesus, and apply it to our lives, we take on our identity as God's children.   In other words, we become like Him because of our original design.   In the book of John Jesus made a statement that caused many of his disciples to leave Him.

<u>John 6:56 – 57</u>
"He that eats my flesh and drinks my blood abides in Me and I in him. As the living Father sent me, and I live because of the Father, so he who feeds on me will live because of me."
NAS

The disciples that left Him that day simply didn't understand what He was talking about. He wasn't speaking in the literal sense of those words, but in the spiritual. He was saying that anyone who would appropriate His blood by faith would receive forgiveness of their sins and would receive the power to live a new life, with a new identity; His life would be hidden with God in Christ Jesus. He would be restored back to His Father's intentions for him and would be blessed greatly by God. He would then be able to enter "boldly" into the very throne room of God, have fellowship with Him and find "help in time of his need and ask for help with the needs of others." The following passage in Luke shows us how powerful it is to pray for others as "blood bought" servants of God in prayer.

Jesus shows us that if we persist in prayer for others, we will eventually get what we ask for.

Luke 11:5

"Which of you shall have a friend, and go to him at midnight and say to him, 'Friend, lend to me three loaves; for a friend of mine has come to me on his journey, and I have nothing to set before him'; and he will answer him from within and say, 'do not trouble me; for the door is now shut; and my children are with me in bed; I cannot rise and give to you'? I say to you though he will not rise to give to him because he is his friend yet because of his persistence he will rise and give him as many as he needs."

Saints of God, it's not because of anything we have done to deserve audience with God. It's because of the positioning of our lives in Christ that we can go to Him on behalf of others and get things they need... salvation, deliverance, and healing! Take advantage of the blood of Jesus and cry out to God on the behalf of others.

Job 22:30

"He will even deliver one who is not innocent; yes, he will be delivered by the purity of your hands."

Then in the words of the Apostle Paul, "I desire therefore that the men to pray everywhere, lifting up holy hands, without wrath and doubting...." (*1st Tim. 2:8*)

Before I close out this chapter I would like to point out one more very powerful truth that I believe has been lost in the last couple of generations of believers. In my earlier days of Christianity I used to hear some of the elderly women in our church tell us to *"plead the blood of Jesus"* over difficult situations. At first I thought this sounded a bit superstitious or archaic at best. *Sorry ladies, but I have since learned the powerful truth behind that principle!*

One commentator defines "*pleading the blood*" as a spiritual dynamic that once understood and applied, releases, delivers and totally annihilates the powers of hell and the flesh and provides safety, protection and release from bondage for the human race.

I see it as our prayers becoming offensive weapons of war against the adversary when we begin to "*plead the blood of Jesus*"!

It's also important to know that "*pleading the blood*" isn't begging and groveling for God to do something! It's more of declaring and believing by faith, with understanding of its efficacy and speaking it forth boldly, knowing that it is backed by the fire and power of our supernatural God that we have come to trust to bring about the desired results!

There is no circumstance in life to which the blood of Jesus isn't a key to God's releasing, protecting and resolving power, whether it is for ourselves or for those we are praying for! "*Pleading the blood of Jesus*" in faith will break the power of sin, witchcraft & rebellion, fear and torment, addiction, shame, and every other force that comes against the human race to keep them in bondage! Because of the spilling of the blood of Jesus, all of mankind's sins have been paid for once and for all!

<u>*Rev. 12:11*</u>

And they overcame him (the adversary/devil) by the blood of the Lamb and by the word of their testimony; and they loved not their lives unto the death.

Hallelujah!

Rev. 5:9

"And they sang a new song, saying: "You (Jesus) are worthy to take the scroll, And to open its seals; for you were slain, and have redeemed us to God by your blood, Out of every tribe and tongue and people and nation, and have made us kings and priests to our God, and we shall reign in the earth."

Nine

The Holy Spirit
Our Heavenly Prayer Partner

In this chapter we are going to talk about the powerful Holy Spirit and how He helps fuel our prayers with passion and power to help us pray through and give birth to the plans, purposes and pursuits of God.

James 5:16b – 18
"The effective, fervent prayer of a righteous man avails much" or as one translation says, "makes much power available, dynamic in its working". Elijah was a man with a nature like ours, and he prayed earnestly that it might not rain; and it did not rain on the earth for three years and six months. And he prayed again, and the sky poured rain, and the earth produced its fruit."

In this passage we are being encouraged to pray until we get results, even though we are mere men just like Elijah and subject to be moved by our many passions. The central truth that we can see if we will look deeper is that we must be fervent for the things of God. When we are, we will hear His voice and pray accordingly as the Holy Spirit directs us to do so. (*If you're not familiar with this particular story about Elijah, read 1 Kings 18.*) Elijah's heart was in tune with God's heart so he prayed earnestly for God's purpose to be fulfilled. He prayed for the rain to stop and start based on a prophetic word given to him by the Lord as He was dealing with Israel.

Many times our prayers aren't earnest or effective simply because we haven't heard the Holy Spirit tell us how to pray according to God's revealed intention. This is why we must learn how to be sensitive to the leading of the Holy Spirit; He will gladly accommodate us! (*Another secret to breaking through in prayer*)

Since the most effective prayers are those lead by the Holy Spirit, let's look at what it takes to make our prayers more effective.

First of all, we must learn to *listen* to the Holy Spirit as we pray.

He's our divine prayer partner. . .

We cannot do anything without Him. He's the one that will help us get our breakthroughs.

Definitions:

Effectual – Gr. *Energeo* – to be active, effective, efficient

Effective – *Webster's* - producing a decisive or desired effect; impressive or striking; ready for service or action; adequate.

Elijah's prayers brought forth the desired results during a very important prophetic season in Israel's history; it was effectual because of the *Holy Spirit* and the *Timing of God*. All Elijah had to do was obey the order. Can we do that today? Yes we can if we've discerned and listened to the voice of the Spirit, not just randomly choose to command it to rain on a hot summer day to see if it works! "Live words", as some have called it, is when the Holy Spirit directs us to speak a certain thing and it will happen. They represent words in our spirit that have freshly been revealed to us. They will definitely get the job done. In the above passage, the prophet prayed for rain and got rain because it was in God's will and His timing, not mans. It was a *"kairos"* time as we've mentioned before; remember - *an opportune time; an appropriate time.* This is why it was effective.

There are a lot of elements involved in effective praying, but the main one is having the power of the Holy Spirit to back you up and manifest the answers. Aimee Semple McPherson, a mighty woman Evangelist, although a controversial figure at times, gives us the key to bringing people to God. Quote: We must be the right *messenger* with the right *message* and have the POWER to deliver it". This is also true in prayer. To be effective in prayer without the Holy Spirit is like trying to bake a good loaf of bread without yeast; it simply won't rise. The Holy Spirit is the only one who can *energize* our prayers. He is the one who keeps us persistent and consistent in prayer. Notice it says, "The effective, fervent prayer".

Fervency – Gr. "*zeo*" - "to be hot"

It implies a *burning desire* to see something happen. Only the Spirit can help us with this type of praying.

In the book of John, Jesus says of the Spirit,

John 14:16 - 26
"And I will ask the Father, and He will give you another 'Helper, that He may be with you forever; that is the Spirit of truth, whom the world cannot receive, because it does not behold Him or know Him, but you know Him because He abides with you and will be in you".

Another - Gr. *Allos* - else - It carries the connotation of sending someone else just like Him to help them finish the work He started.

Helper - Gr. *Parakletos* - an intercessor, consoler: advocate; comforter.

This word is taken from two words, "*Para*" which means alongside and "*Kaleo*" which means to call. He's called along side of us as our Helper or Intercessor.

Intercessor - can also be defined as "one who takes the place of another or one who pleads another's case.

E. Vines Dictionary gives more definition to the word "*Parakletos*". It was used in a court of justice to denote a legal assistant, counsel for the defense, or an advocate; then generally, one who pleads another's cause, an intercessor, advocate. In the widest sense, it signifies a succorer, comforter."

The Amplified Bible translates "*Paraclete*" - (Comforter, Counselor, Helper, Intercessor, Advocate, Strengthener, Standby) This is saying that the Holy Spirit comes along side of us to help us, strengthen us, speak for us, and teach us how to pray. He's our go-between, and our God-connector. He connects us to the main power plant of heaven and makes our prayers effective!

He's our Heavenly Teacher . . .

One of the ways the Holy Spirit helps us is in teaching us spiritual truths.

<u>John 14:26</u>
"But the Helper, the Holy Spirit, whom the Father will send
in My name, he will teach you all things, and bring to your
remembrance all that I have said to you".

Teacher – Gr. *Didasko* – to cause to learn

While Jesus was in the earth, He was the disciples'
teacher, but when He left, the Comforter would be sent to
continue that job.

Paul tells us that his total dependency for his work in
the ministry was placed upon the Holy Spirit working
through him. He says,

<u>1ˢᵗ Cor. 2:1 - 5</u>
"I did not come with superiority of speech or of wisdom,
proclaiming to you the testimony of God; for I determined
to know nothing among you except Christ and Him
crucified. And I was with you in weakness and in fear and
in much trembling. Any my message and my preaching were
not in persuasive words of wisdom but in demonstration of
the Spirit and of power that your faith should not rest on
the wisdom of men, but on the power of God."

Demonstration – Gr. *Apodeixdis* - "manifestation: (unveiling;
a disclosing, revelation).

Paul said his gospel came from the Holy Spirit's power
to reveal or uncover the mysteries that were hidden from the
foundations of the world. He continues in the following:

Vs. 6 - 12

"Yet we do speak wisdom among those who are mature; a wisdom, however, not of this age, nor of the rulers of this age, who are passing away; but we speak God's wisdom in a mystery, the hidden wisdom, which God predestined before the ages to our glory; the wisdom which none of the rulers of this age has understood; for if they had understood it, they would not have crucified the Lord of glory: but just as it is written, 'things which eye has not seen and ear has not heard, and which have not entered the heart of man, all that God has prepared for those who love Him .' For to us God revealed them through the Spirit; for the Spirit searches all things, even the depths of God. For who among men knows the thoughts of a man except the spirit of the man, which is in him? Even so the thoughts of God no one knows except the Spirit of God. Now we have received, not the spirit of the world, but the Spirit who is from God, that we might know the things freely given to us by God."

To try to pray effectively without His help would be futile.

Romans 8:26

"Likewise the Spirit also *helpeth* our *infirmities:* for we know not what we should pray for as we ought: but the Spirit itself (Himself) maketh intercession for us with groaning which cannot be uttered. And He that searches' the hearts knoweth what is the mind of the Spirit, because He maketh intercession for the saints according to the will of God."

Helpeth - Gr. *Sunantilambanomai* - Breaking the Greek word down, we get "*sun*" - together with, "*anti*" - against, "*lambano*" take hold of, which means to "co-operate or assist".

The Holy Spirit *assists* us in praying which makes our prayers effective. He comes to "take hold of whatever it is we are praying for, against anything that is keeping us from obtaining it.

It's very important to know that He will not do it for us, but does it with us. He takes hold together with us against our "infirmities".

Infirmities - Gr. *Astheneia* - "feebleness (of body or mind); Malady; moral frailty: –disease, infirmity, sickness, weakness. One translation of that word is "inability to produce results".

It is the power of the Holy Spirit in us that produces results! Some infirmities may include:

1. *Ignorance* - *"For we know not"* . . .

   In Kenneth Hagin's book <u>The Art of Intercession</u>, he says "ignorance is an infirmity". We don't always know how to pray. So the Holy Spirit, who searches the mind and the heart of God because He knows it, will guide us on how to pray.

   <u>Hosea 4:6</u>
   "My people are destroyed for a lack of knowledge".

   We sometimes have no revelation. The Holy Spirit has to help us "breakthrough" the veil of flesh in prayer and help us discern the will of God. Discern means to be able to fully recognize. As we fully recognize the mind and the heart of God, we are to pray it and God performs it. Things will shift and come to breakthrough! Jesus told us to pray, "Thy Kingdom come, Thy will be done". (*Matthew 6:10*). When we have knowledge of His will, there will be no doubt to hinder us from receiving from Him.

2. *Sickness is an infirmity.*

The Holy Spirit takes hold of the Word of God concerning healing and helps us pray through until we get it. Through intercession empowered by Him, we are penetrating the darkness and bringing about breakthroughs in the spirit realm.

Hebrews 10:35
"Therefore, do not cast away your confidence, which has great reward. For you have need of endurance, so that after you have done the will of God, you may receive the promise....."

The flesh is so weak that it sometimes stops praying just before "breakthrough" comes. It's His job to keep us in the fight long enough to receive from God! He provides the strength and endurance we lack.

3. *Moral weakness is an infirmity.*

The Holy Spirit takes hold of the Word of God that has been planted in us, and helps us pray through when we are tempted to fall. That's why it's so important to stay in prayer when we are weak. He will help us put up a wall of defense around us. How does He do this?

<u>Vs. 26b</u>
"But the Spirit Himself maketh intercession for us with groaning that cannot be uttered".

The Spirit Himself prays through us, for us. He makes intercession. He helps us give *birth* to the plans, purposes and pursuits of God for us as well as those we pray for.

I mentioned earlier that an intercessor was someone who "takes the place of another or one who pleads another's case". Paul tells us that the Holy Spirit in us pleads our case with the Father. Sometimes we don't exactly know how to pray in any given situation because of our infirmities, weaknesses, or inability to discern. God, by the Holy Spirit makes intercession through us as we yield ourselves to Him. The way He does this is through "groaning" or "sighs". J. B. Phillips translation of the Bible calls it, "agonizing longings which cannot be uttered". (*A Secret to Breaking through in Prayer*)

I want to reiterate what I've said before. It is very important to realize that the Holy Spirit does not do our praying for us, but He does it through us as we yield to Him in prayer. Paul said sometimes His intercessions were nothing more than "*groans* which could not be uttered".

Groans – Gr. *Stenagmos* – heavy sighs

Uttered - Gr. - *to articulate* - divided into meaningful parts; intelligible speech; able to express oneself readily and effectively.

In other words, we cannot sometimes interpret our deepest needs or the needs of others. We cannot even express it in words, but as we groan inwardly, it's being interpreted by our God! J. B. Phillips translation of the Bible calls it "agonizing longings which never find words".

We have the Holy Spirit in us and as Paul says, He "searches all things, even the depths of God". (*1st Cor. 2:11*) Part of that "groaning" is the Holy Spirit, joined with our spirit, finding the will of God for us, revealing the will of God to us, and praying the will of God through us! WOW! Paul explains it better in the following passage.

Romans 8:22 - 27

"For we know the whole creation groans and suffers the *pains of childbirth* together until now. (*Secret to Breaking through in Prayer*) And not only this, but also we ourselves, having the first fruits of the Spirit, even we ourselves 'groan within ourselves', waiting eagerly for our adoption as sons, the redemption of our body."

Groan – *another Gr. Sustenazo* - to moan jointly; to experience a common calamity:–groan together.

Notice in that passage, he references the *pains of child birth*.

Child birth – *Heb.* "*travaileth*" – in this case "spiritual birthing"

Spiritual Birthing . . .

Travaileth - *Heb.* "*chuwl* "to have parturition (child birth pain) in company with; to sympathize in expectation of relief from suffering; travail in pain together; to twist or whirl (in a circular or spiral manner), to writhe in pain (especially of parturition); figuratively to wait,-to bear (make to) bring forth, (make to) calve, dance, fall grievously (with pain), to form, be in pain.

What the Holy Spirit is showing us is a very explicit picture of what it's like sometimes to "Agonize in Prayer" to be able to give birth to the plans and purposes of God. He says it's like a woman having a baby. Some preachers don't even like to use the word travail but call it "spiritual birthing". It doesn't sound like fun but the rewards are incredible!

I truly believe that this is one of the things God was talking about in Isaiah when he said that we would be granted "joy" in His house of prayer.

Witnessing the Birth of My Grandson

I had the opportunity of watching my daughter give birth to our grandson, Joshua Michael over 18 years ago. Even though my daughter was the only one experiencing "real pain", believe me, her husband and I were agonizing "with her" in that birthing room. The doctors told us to encourage her a lot and tell her to breathe correctly to help ease some of the pain. Since this was her first baby, she didn't know what to expect. She was afraid and needed assurance. Her labor went on for about 14 hours. I was getting exhausted just looking at her! But her husband and I continued to encourage her. We kept wiping her face with a cool cloth, gave her ice and rubbed her shoulders and arms to help her relax. As the time of birth drew closer, it got pretty intense and we had to continue the coaching. One minister calls the Holy Spirit "our heavenly coach". It's the same in birthing prayers. He's there to help us give birth to the will and purposes of God and encourages us to not give up. She was getting pretty tired and discouraged and thought that the baby was never going to come out, but we continued to coach her, and with the doctor's help, Joshua was born. All the pain left and all the fear of possible complications, etc. completely replaced by the "joy" of seeing Joshua! Praying with the Holy Spirit is like that sometimes.

The word "travaileth" is used again in <u>Isaiah 66:8</u>, to describe the agony the church will go through to give birth to sons and daughters. It reads, "Who hath heard such a thing? Who hath seen such things? Shall the earth be made to bring forth in one day? Or shall a nation be born at once; for as soon as Zion 'travailed' she brought forth her children."

Tying this up, a good interpretation of the Scriptures could mean the following: In prayer . . .

1. We will suffer (*endure pains of childbirth*) in our inner man while we wait for the full redemption of our bodies.

2. We will suffer (*endure pains of childbirth*) until we get more revelation of the fullness of His love towards us.

3. We will suffer (*endure pains of childbirth*) when we recognize that we fall short of His perfection in us.

4. We will suffer (*endure pains of childbirth*) until we are made "complete" in Him.

5. As intercessors, we will suffer (*endure pains of childbirth*) for others to come to the full saving knowledge of the Lord.

It's important to note here that suffering is part of our walk in glory. Jesus said without suffering, there would be no glory. A deeper meaning of the word "suffer" means "to endure pain, hardship or misery". Sometimes I wonder what gospel people have been listening to! Prayer is work and the work is called labor! Need one more Scriptural support? I got it!

<u>Galatians 4:17</u>
"My little children, for whom I *labor* in birth again until Christ is formed in you . . ."

I want you to notice the word "labor" is the Greek word "*odino*" which means "to suffer the pains of childbirth". Notice he said "for whom I labor in birth AGAIN. . . " He didn't just pray for them to get born again, but he also had to continue to pray for them until Christ would be formed in them!

The word "formed" is the Greek word "*morphoo*" and it means "to be fashioned". "To be fashioned" means "to mold, to fit, to construct; to adapt". Because of his prayers of this type, the people he was praying for would not only get born again, but would be molded according to the pattern of Christ! The laboring in prayer is continuous but the results are so worth the price we pay for it.

Ten

Expressions of the Spirit

After discovering some of the *Secrets for Breakthrough in Prayer*, I thought I'd forewarn you that there are many misunderstandings concerning some of the manifestations of the Holy Spirit as we are praying. Groaning, Weeping and Travail are probably the most misunderstood expressions of the Spirit and certainly something we need to clear up and teach properly as it is absolutely necessary for breakthrough.

As I've mentioned before, it's important to remember that the Holy Spirit will not do our praying for us; yes I think this is the 3rd time I've mentioned it, *(just a few hints)* but as we yield to Him, He will express Himself to us and through us. Unless we've yielded to Him and experienced it for ourselves, we might get critical of those who do. I hope the following explanations help if you have been struggling in this area.

Explanations:

1. *Weeping & Compassion*

   The Holy Spirit has many moods and expressions in prayer that quite frankly have either confused many people or drawn them away from *"birthing prayers"* that we briefly discussed in the last chapter, which is part of *intercession.* The very nature of God is expressed through us in prayer.

In prayer, He will express anger, grief, joy, sorrow etc. which all involve emotions.

Rev. Wilford H. Reidt, an intercessor and son in law of John G. Lake says that we enter into the suffering of God through groaning and travail because the "ultimate consciousness of pain resides in God because of His perfect *love* for us". If God is truly in us by His Spirit, we are going to feel what God feels for His creation!

Many times God's compassion would arise in me and I would begin to *weep* for people I didn't even know. This may sound funny, but sometimes well-meaning church people would think it was because I was sad or sorrowful in my life and would come pray for me at the altar. I can assure you I wasn't. We hurt for people in our innermost being because God's love is in us. When we start to pray for them, we sometimes cry because of the compassion of the Lord. Just think about Jesus "*weeping over Jerusalem*". His love was in operation. That's just how love works.

Because God hurts, His love is communicated through us by what I call impressions or expressions of the Holy Spirit.

Impression - *Webster's* - an esp. marked influence or effect or feeling, sense or mind.

The Holy Spirit's influence in our lives will affect us in the emotions. We see it continuously throughout the Ministry of Jesus.

<u>Matthew 9:36</u>
"But when He saw the multitudes, He was moved with
compassion, because they were weary and scattered, like
sheep having no shepherd. Then He said to His
disciples, 'The harvest is plentiful, but the laborers are
few. Therefore pray . . .'"

Compassion – *Webster's* - sympathetic *feeling; pity; mercy*

Compassion is a powerful emotion that compels us to
do something for God. It's the same way in prayer.
What this is saying is that Jesus was stirred in His
emotions to pray for the multitudes.

Please note: We hear a lot about not being led by our
emotions. I agree with that, but we will certainly
experience the Holy Spirit's influence on our emotions.
This many times causes us to take action either by
prayer or by physically helping someone.

2. *Weeping and Silence Before God*

We see this type of praying in Hannah's prayer in <u>1st</u>
<u>Samuel 1</u>. Her desire for a son got so intense, that Eli
the priest at that time thought Hannah was drunk
because he saw her agonizing in prayer at the altar. The
Bible said she was "oppressed in spirit" and was
"praying in her heart" but "*her voice was not heard*". She
was simply giving expression to those "agonizing
longings" that we mentioned before, in her heart and
was so intense about it, that she was mistaken for being
drunk.

Hannah's prayer has been misunderstood by many men and women of God "void "of the Holy Spirit's discernment. We must learn not "to judge by the seeing of the (natural) eye but by the seeing of the (spiritual) eye. (*Isaiah 33:15*) I've even heard some teach that she was in doubt and unbelief because she was crying at the altar and should have just confessed it, believed it and that would have settled it. Well, it doesn't always work that way. Confession of the promises of God is certainly part of the battle, but sometimes there will be intense times of deep lamentation with *quietness before God*. This is part of *intercession* that many of us have a problem understanding. Through Hannah's lamentation in quietness before God, her victory was won. It seemed that God was pleased with her time at the altar because He eventually answered her prayers and gave her a son. Eli was even convinced and pronounced the victory before she left. SELAH

1st Samuel 1:19b
"And Elkanah (Hannah's husband) had relations with Hannah his wife, and the Lord remembered her. And it came about in due time, after Hannah had conceived, that she gave birth to a son; and she named him Samuel, saying, 'because I have asked him of the Lord.'"

I believe that Hannah's desire for a son came from God and she was empowered by God to "bring it forth or give birth to it". Scripture tells us that even though the Old Testament saints did not have the benefits of having the Holy Spirit in them, they were definitely led and empowered by Him to bring forth their promises.

3. *Loud Weeping or Wailing and Lamentation*

This is the type of praying that really gets people either upset or afraid that something weird is going on! There are great benefits to "weeping and wailing" when God is the author of it. If the Holy Spirit can be grieved like Paul teaches us in <u>Ephesians 4:30</u>, then He certainly is entitled to cry. This is perhaps the most misunderstood way that the Holy Spirit moves upon us in *travail*. Many times the Holy Spirit has moved upon me and thousands of other intercessors, with loud weeping and wailing, especially for the salvation of loved ones or those who were facing an urgent crisis situation.

In Jeremiah's day, as we've mentioned in a previous chapter, God anointed that Prophet by moving upon him with *weeping* and *travail*. (*Jeremiah 8:18*) It said "His sorrow was beyond healing; . . . He was broken, he was mourning and dismay had totally taken hold of him He continues: "Is there no balm in Gilead? Is there no physician there? Why then has not the health of the daughter of my people been restored?" There is more crying to come!

<u>Jeremiah 9:1</u>
"Oh that my head were waters, and my eyes a fountain of tears that I might weep day and night for the slain of the daughter of my people!"

What was happening to Jeremiah? I've heard different ministers say that Jeremiah was depressed and was simply a "cry baby". If they only knew by saying what they said only proved to show how ignorant they were, they probably wouldn't have said it!

Weeping Misunderstood!

I was at a meeting in OK when a fellow minister was asked to say what the Holy Spirit was saying to him at that time. He got up and began to speak the word of the Lord and the compassion of the Lord hit him like a wave and he began to weep for the youth of our nation. Those of us in the service were so moved by the Holy Spirit that we all began to weep. To me, it was a sovereign move of the Spirit. To the one in charge who had asked him to speak, it was an opportunity to rebuke the brother in front of the entire congregation and told him crying wasn't necessary anymore because God already had a plan.

I'm sorry if this sounds critical but that was spiritual ignorance. I heard he later apologized to the brother because there was such opposition to what He had done!

The prophet Jeremiah was sharing in the sufferings of God for that generation in his prayers just as my brother was sharing the sufferings of God for the youth of our nation! The burden became so intense and more than he could handle alone that Jeremiah issued a call to the women to come and help him. *(Jeremiah 9:17)*

Something powerful happens when people are moved upon by God to weep. In Jeremiah's day, God wanted them to *weep* in repentance for revival for their nation.

In Nehemiah's day he was found fasting and *weeping* in repentance for the sins of his nation. This is called *"sowing in tears..."*

Psalms 126:5, 6
"Those who sow in tears shall reap with joyful shouting.
He, who goes to and fro weeping, carrying his bag of
seed, Shall indeed come again with a shout of joy,
bringing his sheaves with him".

Jesus also sowed in tears . . .

Hebrews 5:7
"In the days of His flesh, He offered up both prayers
and supplications with loud crying and tears . . ."

How many of you know that God answered Jesus'
prayers? As I've mentioned, many times this type of
expression has been misunderstood and written off as "too
emotional" but *weeping* has its purpose and it needs to have
its place. I realize that there have been excesses of the flesh
to contend with, but I know many good, sound intercessors
that have been labeled as "fruits, nuts and flakes" by men
and women of God, who like Eli, didn't have enough
discernment to fully understand what was going on. Many
times they were "shut down" and made to feel like they had
done something wrong when they yielded to that type of
praying. Let's get some wisdom!

Why are we so threatened by emotions? The problem
with a lot of us is that we haven't been taught healthy ways
to release what we feel, so we are told to stifle it. Men are
taught not to cry; it's a sign of weakness. But if we're going
to enter into effective intercession, we are going to have to
yield to the expressions of the Holy Spirit which sometimes
involve crying and *lamentation.*

I cannot move forward until I say this and I'm going to say it with all the love and patience I can muster. Many intercessors say that all we need do in prayer is prophecy, declare and decree and God will establish those things we are praying for. While this is true, we cannot forget that some fields have not been watered in prayer with weeping and lamentation so we really need to hear what the Spirit says to do and then we'll really see the powerful manifestations of God!

Let me share one more recent encounter that prevented the Holy Spirit from moving forward in this kind of praying.

A Move of the Spirit Abruptly Interrupted

Last year I attended an Awakening Event in OK and was greatly disturbed at what I witnessed as one of the speakers was talking about the love and concern God had for a particular state. It was obvious that as he continued to speak, the Holy Spirit moved on several men, yes I said men, and one by one they came up to the altar in response to this sovereign move of God. They all simultaneously began to fall on their faces; broken and unashamedly weeping before the Father for the sins of that particular state. Many who were seated around us sensed what was going on and also began to pray, along with several women who were with me. All of a sudden we were abruptly interrupted by a person speaking over the microphone, making announcements that it was time for the next speaker. Everything stopped instantly. I was grieved in my heart as I'm sure others were also. How many times are we going to interrupt God with our own programs and time limits? A righteous anger came over me. What? We can't kneel and pray for the people in that state because we have a list of speakers to get to?

It got very quiet and someone asked if I had anything to say! I guess I had a hard time covering up how I felt! At first I thought, I'm just a guest here and I don't want to be negative but God checked my heart and said speak. I got up and shared that we had grieved the Holy Spirit and a few other things about that and hoped we would all try to get more intimately acquainted with Him in order to recognize when He was moving. I also said that we needed to remember what really needed to be accomplished by our gatherings. It got very quiet and the group was very pensive.

All the way back to my room at lunch break, I kicked myself for speaking it out. Why did I have to do that Lord? I feel like a trouble maker! I almost didn't even go back to the afternoon session, but I was so glad I did. While standing at the table getting water, one of the men who had been drawn to the altar that morning came up to me and asked if he could talk to me for a minute. (*By the way, he was part of the leadership team of that Awakening Meeting*) I could tell he'd been crying and was very sober about what he wanted to say.

First of all he thanked me for sharing the truth the way I did and that it became very clear to him that the Holy Spirit had been leading him for a long time to weep for the spiritual condition of our nation, but somehow he was always interrupted. He knew in his heart that the Holy Spirit was grieved each time and wished he would have addressed it. I could tell he was still very broken to the point of tears because they had made no room for that kind of expression that morning, and were more concerned about their agenda. He told me he went back to his room and finished the work that was started at the altar that morning! Wow! This was truly a man after God's own heart! I was very blessed that this man of God shared this with me. He said he was also going to share it with the others because he finally got clarity on the importance of following the leading of the Holy Spirit.

Lamentation

Other times, *lamentation* and *sorrow* have come up from my belly (spirit) as I prayed for certain people who were hurting or perhaps rebelling against God. It was intense and very sorrowful. When the Holy Spirit moves us to pray for people, sometimes His desire for them is mixed with feelings of their intense need and desperation.

Lament - *Webster's* - to cry aloud in grief; to mourn aloud; to wail; to express sorrow or regret"

I will never forget the funeral of a little six month old baby in Colby, KS. It was my husband's first funeral to ever preach. We had to go to the funeral home and be with the mother and father when they viewed their little baby for the first time since its death. The funeral director decided to let the mother hold the baby before they placed its little body in the casket. I shall never forget the *lament* of that mother when she held her dead baby! She unashamedly expressed her deep sorrow and agony with loud crying and wailing that came from deep within her spirit. My husband and I cried with them and held on to each other like it had been our baby that died. We shared in their grief with them.

The Holy Spirit has moved upon me with this type of lamentation multiple times; none of it being pleasant I might add. I was just a yielded vessel He could use to pray for a serious situation involving loss. It's one of the ways we "suffer" with Him for His creation. I've had this type of lamentation for lost loved ones who are going the wrong way. Sometimes, it was accompanied with deep regret and mourning knowing that some of them would say "no" to God and were going to suffer severely for it.

While some of these expressions of the Holy Spirit can cause misunderstandings and possibly strike fear in baby Christians, there still needs to be place for it. My solution to this problem is for churches to have rooms available for their intercessors to go to when this happens. When it happens at home, find a private place to release those expressions. It will definitely be worth it in the long run. Remember, it's the moving of the Spirit when that happens! We mustn't shut down this type of praying.

Important to Note: If we take away the tears from the altars of our churches like many have done all we will have left is a "form of religion, void of the power".

An Urgent Departure to Pray

I remember a time in church when God moved upon the heart of my friend Anna to intercede this way. The burden was so strong, that she started crying right in the middle of the service we were attending. She looked at me with tears rolling down her face and I knew something was very wrong! A very close friend of hers, who was not saved, had suddenly come to her mind and she knew he was in danger and needed to release the burden of the Lord. We both knew it was not going to be pretty or appropriate for sure! We decided she needed to quickly find a room to release the burden as it was coming on her like a women in labor!

She found a room and hit the floor with loud weeping and wailing asking God to spare this person and bring him home safely. There's really no other way to describe this but it comes from a very deep place in our Spirit and comes with an urgent thrust that you know it's not you. Then, just as fast as it came, it left. She knew something powerful had just happened for her friend. She later found out that his life was spared in a very serious boating accident that had taken place at the exact time she was moved by the Holy Spirit to pray!

She recently revealed to me that while she was praying someone came to the door and quickly shut the door because they felt the power of God so strong that they knew something holy/private was going on! God is so awesome!

The Bible teaches in <u>2nd Chron. 16:9</u> that "the eyes of the Lord run to and fro throughout the whole earth, to show Him strong on behalf of those whose heart is loyal towards Him". He can do this, not only for us but for others if we yield to Him in prayer!

Another important thing to understand about this type of praying is that it can come upon you without warning. Many times while driving my car, I've had to pull over to the side of the road to release what came bubbling up out of my heart as I prayed with the Spirit. He would bring to mind certain people that needed this type of intercession.

I remember back in the 80's, every time I saw a school bus, I would begin to weep and wail in intercession for the children on that bus. For a while back then, I thought I'd never get through a day without this happening, especially when I'd drop my children off at school. Eventually, it subsided and I felt as if God had seen the days ahead for the children of our nation and released intercession for them through a yielded vessel. Then there were other times I'd turn the television on and when I would pass the Music Television channel, I would begin to weep and travail for those young people to get saved. Does this happen to me all the time? The answer is no. But it does happen. When it does, I know it's not "worked up" so I yield to it and it brings great blessing, because God is in it.

There's been lot's of *error* concerning this type of praying. If people try to "work it up" every time they go to prayer, it's what I call a "false burden" and it becomes nothing more than human emotions. Many good intercessors have fallen prey to this when they were first learning to yield to the Holy Spirit. It then becomes "exhibition" and gets them labeled as "weird or strange" and thwarts the purposes of God for the "true expressions" of the Holy Spirit to flow in order to bring great blessing to those we are praying for. A good rule of thumb to help keep us balanced in this area is to remember "Weeping or sorrow may last for the night, but joy comes in the morning". (*Psalms 30:5*)

A few more examples and I'll move forward to the next chapter.

A Night of Eminent Danger

I remember one time in particular, I had my parents over for dinner and I was right in the middle of fixing the meat sauce for a pot of spaghetti I was making for them, when all of a sudden, an overwhelming sadness and grief, coupled with tears began to flow up from my belly. I didn't

141

really understand what this was, (*I was still very young in the Lord*) but I had to excuse myself and run to my prayer closet. The Holy Spirit showed me that my daughter's life was in danger. She had gone with her father and grandfather on a fishing expedition in the Gulf of Mexico that weekend. As the burden intensified, I began to weep and wail at the top of my lungs for God to show me what was happening, but He didn't. All I knew is that they were all in danger. This agonizing and weeping in prayer along with deep intercession went on quite some time and at midnight I just put it in God's hands and tried to rest. My parents, of course, thought I was losing my mind. They were frightened and at first, so was I. I knew it was God and that He was going to take care of the situation.

Since I couldn't sleep, I worshipped God and prayed as best as I could. I struggled even though I knew God was intervening and things were going to be all right. My spirit was at peace, but I continued to wrestle with fear in my mind. Little did I know until the morning, what had been accomplished through my prayers! I'll let my daughter, Natalie, tell you.

"My dad, grandfather, and his wife Sue were fishing about fifty (50) miles off the Louisiana coast in the Gulf of Mexico. What we expected to be a quick fishing trip turned into a two-day event. We had planned to go back inland the same day we went out, but noticed towards late afternoon that the bilge pump on our boat had gone out. Because of the lateness of the hour, we didn't want to take any chances of having to navigate in Gulf waters at night, so we hooked our anchor to a jack up barge and decided to spend the night and radio for help in the morning.

For those of you who don't know what a jack-up barge is, I'll explain. It's a self propelled, self-contained oil field equipment/crane work vessel that is shaped like a barge. It has navigation equipment on it, and has 3 to 4 legs that are anywhere from 30 to 70 feet in height. These legs are used to jack up and level the barge during work operations and sometimes during rough sea conditions when en route. Thank God we had it to tie our boat to.

When it got dark, my grandfather and his wife went down into the cabin to sleep. I laid down on the bench outside and my dad on the bench opposite me. He was keeping watch. I remember not being able to fall asleep that night because the waves were so high and I was getting sick to my stomach.

We had found out earlier that there was another boat on the other side of the jack up barge and had notified them by radio of our plight. We asked them to stay on the same radio frequency in case we needed them.

At about midnight, I awoke to my dad screaming, "we're going down – get out of the boat"! I jumped up, got on the radio and yelled 'we're sinking, we're sinking'! Water was coming in so fast that it took about 3 seconds for me to be up to my waist in water. My dad was yelling at me to get a knife for something, but I couldn't understand the rest of what he was saying. Our boat was sinking bottom first!

I heard the screams of my grandfather and his wife as they were struggling to get out of the cabin downstairs, but couldn't get out through the door because of the water pressure. They were trying to squeeze through a very tiny cabin window. Sue couldn't swim so she had put on a very bulky life jacket which kept her from being able to go through the window. The harder she struggled, the more she panicked. At that moment I thought Sue was not going to make it and my Grandfather, who had gone through two heart surgeries, was going to have a heart attack.

Our boat sank in a matter of ten (10) seconds, tops! I had just gotten the knife that my dad was asking for and after handing it to him, I was under water! In the process of grabbing the knife for him, I had gotten my ankle tangled up in one of our deep sea fishing lines. When I tried to come up, I couldn't. The line was stuck to the pole in the boat. That's how fast your life can pass before your eyes! After what seemed like eternity, I felt this huge hand grab me by my shirt collar and pull me up, fishing pole and all! It was my dad. He saved my life. My nose was bleeding very badly, I guess from the pressure and I could still hear the screams of my grandfather and his wife.

We had a small Boston Whaler on top of our yacht, but we couldn't use it because it flipped upside down and we couldn't get in it. The men who were fishing on the other side of the jack-up barge finally got to us and picked me up out of the water. They then helped my dad pull my grandfather and Sue out of the sunken boat cabin.

The next thing that happened was that we were lifted up into the jack-up barge by a crane, one at a time, and spent the night there. We were truly a sight! Scared, wet, cold and exhausted! And I forgot - - thankful. Coming that close to death, I realized how precious life is. It really put the fear of God in me. My grandfather and his wife have died since that event, but lived many years to tell the story because they had a praying mom also! I know if my mom hadn't prayed, it would not have turned out as good as it did!

I believe, like my daughter, that if I hadn't yielded myself to the Holy Spirit's impressions and allowed Him to express Himself through me, things would not have turned out as wonderful as they did! God was able to intervene and save lives because of the intercession to do so!

Stay Close to God

I wish that all my stories were as powerful as that one, and turned out as wonderful, but unfortunately, they were not. There were plenty of times in my life when I wasn't walking as closely with God as I should have been and I wasn't as sensitive to His leading in that type of praying. We must *stay close to God* and get informed about the things of God so we can move forward victoriously. Sometimes in this life we will still experience hardship but if we stay close to God and alert to His promptings, we will experience less and less and also stay strong when our prayers aren't answered in the way we want them to be!

I'd read the following passage of Scripture before, but I didn't know the depth of what my family and I would have to walk through.

Romans 8:28
". . . and we know that God causes all things to work together for good, to those who love God, to those who are the called according to His purpose."

One morning I went off to work as I did every day at 8:00 a.m., only this time I had to leave my 14 year old son at home alone. He had gotten suspended from school for talking to two guys who were smoking on the school ground.

In a meeting with his principal, I tried to reason with him to please let him go to school and punish him some other way because I was a single mom and had to work. I also said he wasn't the one smoking but they wouldn't hear of it. He said this incident would be used as an example of what happens to kids when they smoke or hang around with kids who did or broke other rules.

When I left that morning I began to feel a sense of foreboding about the whole deal and really didn't know what to do. Since he usually listened to me and had never gotten into trouble before, I figured it was going to be alright, but the uneasiness wouldn't leave. When I got to work I called him and told him not to leave the house and that I would call him later. The feelings wouldn't go away. I called the house again on my break and this time got no answer. My worst fears were being confirmed, but instead of getting permission to leave in order to go check on him or find a place to pray, I stayed and was tormented with this deep sense of dread and danger for my son as I sat paralyzed at the switchboard!

I couldn't bring myself to tell anyone what was going on so I asked to take an early lunch and went looking for him. He wasn't home and since we were new in that area, I had no idea where to even look for him. I drove back to the office and was going to tell my boss I was leaving when I saw a policeman in the foyer looking for me. He told me my son had been shot by one of his friends in an accident involving a 30-30 deer rifle, and was on the way to the hospital. His face was very grave and I knew he didn't think he was going to make it. I cannot put into words the shock I felt at that moment. I immediately heard these words like someone was standing right beside me, "He will live and not die" coupled with "what Satan has done for harm I will turn it around and use it for good, to save many people." Please don't misunderstand. God did not do this for some weird purpose of His, but He takes the bad things that happen to us and can use it for our good. (*Genesis 50:20*)

My son had gone over to the house of one of the boys that got suspended to play video games and eat pizza. The young man pulled out a rifle from his father's collection that he had purchased to go deer hunting and showed it to the boys. He did not know it was loaded and accidently fired the gun, shooting my son at close range in the right arm at the elbow. Being a high-powered deer rifle, the damage was devastating.

My son remembers his friends running away in fear; the boy of the father who owned the gun was found in a fetal position under the bed and the other one ran away. By the time he realized what happened, my son dialed emergency 911 services for himself, before passing out on the lawn in the front yard!

The medics that arrived told me that one of them was a Christian and as he prepped him he prayed for him and spoke these words over him, "You will live and not die and declare the glory of the Lord". I was also told that upon his arrival at the hospital, a nurse who was put in charge in the E.R. that day prayed over him speaking the exact same promise "you will live and not die and declare the glory of the Lord"! Even though he had lost eight (8) pints of blood, God was watching over him and preserved his life.

He survived that horrific accident and had to undergo several surgeries. Even though the re-attachment was successful, his team of doctors told me that he would not be able to gain complete use of His arm because he was missing a radial nerve necessary for mobility. I thanked them but refused the report! I didn't know it at the time, but I was given the *gift of faith* to believe that God not only *could* but *would* completely restore the use of his arm.

During the surgery, I remember lying on the bathroom floor in the E.R. waiting room; a place I don't recommend you lying on, but I didn't care. As I prayed to God I realized that he belonged to God before he belonged to me and was a gift. I later recognized that in my prayer I had laid my youngest son on the altar, (*another secret to breakthrough*) totally surrendering him to the one who created him. I let the Lord know that I knew He was in charge of life and death; and things pertaining to Ryan's life and whether or not his arm could be reattached successfully and be returned to its full use. It was a very *private/secret/solemn* moment and I knew God and His angels were listening. I listened for His voice after that extreme travail and knew he was going to be healed. I dried my eyes, got up with faith in my heart and faced the trial, fully trusting in the Lord.

Throughout the whole ordeal God did many *miracles* and I'm eternally grateful. He did restore the use of his arm and hand! For a long time I wrestled in my heart because I knew the Holy Spirit was trying to warn me of impending danger. I asked myself so many times if this attack could have been possibly averted had I yielded in prayer to get instructions from the Lord. People have told me not to blame myself but to give glory to God. All of us at best are still flawed human beings and sometimes we miss it; I don't blame myself anymore but it's simply by the *grace* of God. Wisdom has taught me to move forward and trust God. The enemy uses weapons against us and our children to "kill - steal - destroy", but I'm thankful for my faithful heavenly Father Who came through for us.

I do believe if we'd learn to yield to the promptings of the Holy Spirit, a lot of things that Satan has planned for destruction would be averted. Let's not through ignorance or fear of the unknown, ignore the promptings of the Holy Spirit any longer. Our prayer should be, "Father, make me sensitive to your Spirit's promptings so that I can be used in prayer to do what I can to stop the enemy dead in his tracks!"

Oh, by the way, my son is a self taught resin artist showing and selling the most exquisite pieces of art at this time, in the Beaudry Gallery in Dallas, TX. What a gift and what a faithful God! Just recently we were able to meet with his doctor after 26 years and thank him again for the tremendous job he and his team of doctors did for my son. He visited Ryan at the gallery here in Dallas. We were so blessed to see him and his lovely wife!

Angelic Response to Prayer

I knew I was not going to get out of this chapter without sharing one more glorious story! This one is about my urgent praying for my oldest son who had gotten on drugs after his father left us, and God's *response to my prayers!*

I was sleeping one night after a season of prayer and travail for him, and was suddenly awakened by someone tugging very hard at my toes! I couldn't see very clearly but what I saw frightened me at first. It was a very large figure standing at the foot of my bed urging me to get up and run after my son. I was stunned and shocked to say the least! Yes, it was an angel; a very large and in charge angel at that.

He said to me "get up and get up now, your oldest son has run away. He has climbed out of his bedroom window and will be in grave danger unless he is rescued! At that point he gave me instructions and told me *exactly* where to go in detail!

I shot up out of the bed and ran to my son's bedroom. The window was wide open and the curtains where blowing in the cold wind. I then ran to my other son's room and he was asleep like a baby. The words came back to me as I grabbed my coat without even changing out of my pajamas, "he will be in grave danger unless he is rescued". I slipped on my boots and jumped into the car. I knew I wasn't on my own but that God had sent help and I was on His GPS system. Without even realizing what I was doing I drove right up to the place and saw my son on a payphone outside of a convenience store trying to hook up with some older guys to buy drugs.

I wish I had a picture of my son's face as he turned around and saw his mom sitting in the car. He slammed the phone down and got into the car, and was very angry as we drove home. All the way there he yelled and screamed and said "how did you know where I was"? He was in "shock" and I was in "awe" of what God did for us that night. I believe he might have gotten the wrong kind of drugs or encountered some really dangerous people in the process. He was hurt, angry and disappointed at the way things turned out in our family. Seeing his pain as he knocked holes in the garage walls was overwhelming! He was angry and crying and so was I. I called my pastor and he came to try and help us. It was a very uphill climb since then and year's later things still aren't where they should be, but God is still hearing my prayers!

One more thing to remember, we don't determine the outcome of our prayers, (*another secret to breakthrough*) but we learn to trust God as He hears them and releases His plan (*not ours*) to redeem those people and situations we are praying for.

Eleven
What about Praying in the Spirit?

We certainly cannot talk about the Holy Spirit and prayer without talking about the Baptism of the Holy Spirit with the evidence of speaking in tongues; another way to describe it is called praying in the Spirit. Why this is so controversial simply baffles me but it is one of the "*Secrets to Breaking through in Prayer.*" When I came to the Lord at age 29 I simply believed everything I read in the Bible. I had spent too many years believing what man taught me in the denomination I grew up in. I wanted to hear what God had to say about things that I saw in His word. My final deduction is "if it's in the word of God – I want it"!

Therefore, those of you who truly want everything God has to offer will enjoy this portion of teaching. Others will probably stop reading the book because of erroneous teaching that "tongues are not for today" or "they're from the devil", etc. I submit to you that it is estimated as of 2016 that over 500 Billion people have received the empowering of the Holy Spirit, also known as the Baptism in the Holy Spirit with the evidence of speaking in other tongues since the Azusa Street Revival! The Baptism of the Holy Spirit was also prophesied by Isaiah; given an honorable mention by Jesus in the book of Mark and was demonstrated by the mighty Holy Spirit in the Book of Acts. I hope all of you reading up to this point will continue to be open to such a glorious experience.

In the Book of Acts, believed to have been written by the Apostle Luke, Jesus told those who had gathered in the upper room why they need to be baptized in the Holy Spirit.

Acts 1:4 – 8

"And, being assembled together with them, commanded them that they should not depart from Jerusalem, but wait for the promise of the Father, which saith he, ye have heard of me. For John truly baptized with water; but ye shall be baptized with the Holy Ghost not many days hence. Then they therefore were come together, they asked of him, saying, Lord, wilt thou at this time restore again the kingdom to Israel? And he said unto them, it is not for you to know the times or the seasons, which the Father hath put in His own power. But ye shall receive *power,* after that the Holy Ghost is come upon you; and ye shall be witnesses unto me both in Jerusalem, and in all Judaea, and in Samaria, and unto the uttermost part of the earth."

Power – Gr. *Dynamis* – strength, power, ability; power for performing miracles, moral power and excellence of soul, etc.

Being baptized in the Holy Spirit as we can now see, is not only about speaking in tongues but about having the power of the Spirit to work the workings of God and be His authentic witnesses with signs following.

Most Christians call this the Baptism in the Holy Spirit or being filled with the Holy Spirit.

Acts 10:44 - 46

"While Peter was still speaking these words, the Holy Spirit fell upon all those who were listening to the message. And all the circumcised believers who had come with Peter were amazed, because the gift of the Holy Spirit had been poured out upon the Gentiles also, for they were hearing them *speaking with tongues* and exalting God."

Acts 2:3

"Then there appeared to them, divided tongues, as of fire, and one sat upon each of them. And they were all filled with the Holy Spirit and began to speak with other tongues, as the Spirit gave them utterance."

Again we see this in *Acts 19* where the apostle Paul finds a group of disciples in Ephesus who had been baptized in water, but had never been baptized in the Holy Spirit.

Acts 19

"And it came about that while Apollos was at Corinth, Paul having passed through the upper country came to Ephesus, and found some disciples, and he said to them, 'Did you receive the Holy Spirit when you believed?' And they said to him, 'No, we have not even heard whether there is a Holy Spirit.' And he said, 'Into what then were you baptized?' And they said, 'Into John's baptism.' And Paul said, 'John baptized with the baptism of repentance, telling the people to believe in Him who was coming after him, that is, in Jesus.' And when they heard this, they were baptized in the name of the Lord Jesus. And when Paul laid his hands upon them, the Holy Spirit came upon them, and they began speaking with tongues and prophesying."

To say it simply, tongues are the sign that God has come on the scene. It's God's way, not man's way of manifesting Himself to us and should be the initial sign that should follow all believers.

Mark 16:14 – 20

And He (Jesus) said to them, "Go into the entire world and preach the gospel to every creature. He who believes and is baptized will be saved; but he who does not believe will be condemned. And these signs will follows them that believe: In my name they will cast out demons; they will speak with new tongues; they will take up serpents (sicknesses and diseases); and if they drink anything deadly, it will by no means hurt them; they will lay hands on the sick and they will recover."

Well, that makes it pretty plain. If we believe it, we will experience it. If we don't, we won't! So let's go on. If you've gotten this far and haven't put the book down, you're doing great! God will show himself strong if you will only believe.

First of all, tongues are a very valid part of enjoying the presence of God in a believer's life, and a very valid tool for interpreting the heart and mind of God in prayer. I want you to notice that every time the experience is mentioned, the recipients were found "magnifying and glorifying God" and "great joy would flood the cities". (*Acts 2:11, Acts 10:46, Acts 8:8 & Acts 13:52*) Guys, this can't be bad! The Scripture says that the "kingdom of God is righteousness, peace and joy....*in the Holy Spirit*" In fact, joy is the end result of our travail as we mentioned in the last chapter. If you are a Believer and are not baptized in the Holy Spirit, I encourage you to believe God and take Him at His word concerning this subject. Get some good books by reputable authors who have had this experience, and ask the Lord to baptize you in the Holy Spirit. You will begin to experience God in ways you've never been able to before, and your life will drastically change for the better.

So what about these tongues as they relate to prayer? The Bible teaches that when we pray in tongues, "we are not speaking to men, but to God; for no one understands, but in his spirit (man's spirit) he speaks mysteries." (*1ˢᵗ Cor. 14:2*) The apostle Jude teaches that praying in our prayer language "builds us up" and makes us strong. (*Jude 21*) The Apostle Paul teaches the same thing but uses the word "edify".

1 Cor. 14:4
"One who speaks in a tongue edifies himself . . ."

Edify – *Gr. oikodomeo*" to be a house builder, that is to construct or figuratively, to confirm.

What God is saying through this teaching is that when we pray in this heavenly language, we are constructing our spiritual house!   Another way to say it is that God's Word is being confirmed to us in our inner man or our spirit man. I like to refer to the following passage of Scripture when speaking on this subject found in the book of Proverbs.

Proverbs 20:27
"The spirit of a man is the candle or lamp of the Lord, searching all the inner depths of his heart."

God reveals things to a man in his heart or his spirit, not his head. People have tried to gain understanding of the Baptism in the Holy Spirit through their intellect or reasoning faculties. That's not going to work. The gospel of Jesus Christ is not a gospel of head learning, but of the heart and is to be taken by faith. The writer of the Book of Hebrews says it's "by faith we understand that the worlds were prepared by the word of God . . ." (*Hebrews 11:3*) It's only by faith that we believe tongues is a very valid part of our prayer life and it's the witness of the Spirit that gives us understanding in our hearts that the experience is still for today and it is a valid gift from God.

Romans 8:15 & 16
"For you have not received the spirit of bondage again to
fear; but ye have received the Spirit of adoptions, whereby
we cry Abba Father. The Spirit Himself bears witness with
our spirit that we are children of God . . . "

When a believer is born of God's Spirit, the Holy Spirit,
as I've said before, bears witness with them of who they are.
When a believer is baptized in the Holy Spirit and prays in
his/her heavenly language, the Holy Spirit gives them *power*
to receive what belongs to them in Christ Jesus. These are
two (2) separate experiences that must be realized by
Believers seeking understanding. Look what the following
passage says about this:

1ˢᵗ Cor. 2:10, 12 & 13
"For to us God revealed them through the Spirit; for the
Spirit searches all things, even the depths of God. "Now we
have received, not the spirit of the world, but the Spirit who
is from God, that we might know the things freely given to
us by God, which things we also speak, not in words taught
by human wisdom, but in those taught by the Spirit,
combining spiritual thoughts with spiritual words".

What does all that mean?

It's so important to understand what he said about
"*speaking forth mysteries*". What are these *mysteries*?

Mysteries – Gr. *musterion* - *divine secrets* or "the things freely
given to us by God". The connotation is that only those
who are initiated by God, or we should say, has His Spirit,
can have these secrets revealed to them!

In *Luke 12*, Jesus said it was the "Father's good pleasure to gives us the Kingdom". In other words, to reveal things about the kingdom that others don't know.

Matthew 11:25

"I praise Thee, O Father, Lord of heaven and earth, that Thou didst hide these things from the wise and intelligent and didst reveal them to babes. Yes, Father, for thus it was well pleasing in your sight".

How does God do this? He does it by *revelation*. The Kingdom of God is not built on information, but on *revelation*.

Revelation – Gr. *Apokolysis* – Laying bare; a disclosure of truth; the making known of something that was previously secret or unknown

Man cannot give us *revelation*. In *Matthew 16:15-16* Jesus asked Peter "who do men say that I am?" Peter answered and said "thou art the Christ, the Son of the Living God." Jesus answered him and said "Thou art blessed Simon Barjona: for flesh and blood hath not revealed this to you, but my father who is in heaven." Only His Spirit can reveal these things to us in our heart. As we pray in our prayer language and study His word, the Holy Spirit is able to reveal things to our spirit man, and we become strong in the Lord and built up in His truth.

Romans 10:17

"So faith comes by hearing and hearing by the word (*rhema or revealed word*) of God."

As we pray in tongues the Holy Spirit speaks forth these *mysteries*; how the kingdom of God works, who we are in Christ; secrets to breaking through in prayer, etc. Our spirit picks this up, gives understanding to our minds and we are strengthened and made able to move forward by His power. That is why Paul said "he prayed with his spirit and with the understanding". The Holy Spirit was the One who gave him the understanding of what his spirit was praying! (*1 Cor. 14:13 & 14*) No wonder the devil tries to keep this experience out of the hands of the saints!

Please don't confuse your own heavenly prayer language with the gift of tongues found in *1st Cor. 12:10*, "*divers kinds of tongues*" especially if you're going to make the argument against speaking in tongues all together. These tongues or generally used for public demonstration and in need of an "interpretation" so that the body of Christ can be built up. This does not mean that you will never pray in a "known tongue" in your prayer life because you will; especially if you are praying for other nations. We are simply instructed not to do it in a public way. Paul is very clear when he says it's better to prophesy in public than to speak in one of those "various kinds of tongues" when there is no one to interpret.

When Paul tells us to pray in our heavenly language for our own personal edification, this is totally different from speaking in other tongues to edify the body of Christ. The only way to know the difference is to actually experience it. Some things cannot be explained. After all, who can explain how the Spirit of God heals people; yet He does.

If you ask people how He did it, they usually don't know. All they know is that He did.

There are plenty of ways the Holy Spirit prays through us; for ourselves and for others that still remain a mystery to me and probably if we all were to admit it, we are not going to know everything there is no know about this magnificent God! The following is a beautiful example of praying in a known tongue at a prayer meeting.

Praying for Scandinavia

I had the opportunity to attend a Pastor's wives conference in Houston, TX. I was not a pastor's wife at that time, but my friend got "clearance" so to speak, for me to attend the conference. It just so happened to be one of the most eye opening conferences I had ever attended; some very positive and awe-inspiring things and some just really sad, especially when I got to hear about the pain and suffering these women were going through in their churches.

One night we gathered as usual to pray for the nations. I was at the altar yielding my spirit to the Holy Spirit. I began praying in a tongue that was not familiar to me at all. It was different than my normal prayer language. One of the speakers on the platform heard me and came over to me with tears in her eyes, amazed at what I was praying. She tapped me lightly on the shoulder and asked me if I was Scandinavian? I told her no. She said she was and that I was praying in her Scandinavian language. She said I was asking the God of heaven, over and over again, to send sweet bread to the people of Scandinavia because His people there really loved him. I remember crying because I was so moved by her response. This woman was really touched by that gift in operation and asked me to come up to the platform and share what had just happened! Of course I did and the place exploded with wonder and amazement at how

God works in His people! She left that meeting knowing the people of Scandinavia were on God's heart! What a report she would bring back to them! I left there honored that God had used me to bring blessings to someone else while praying!

What does it take to be baptized in the Holy Spirit with the evidence of speaking/praying in tongues? It takes faith, beloved; simple, child-like faith. You can receive it no other way. You must clear your heart of any obstacles such as unbelief, erroneous teaching, fear or whatever else is in your way of receiving.

The Scriptures says that Jesus is the one "who will baptize you with the Holy Spirit and with fire". (*Matthew 3:11*) Anything that Jesus does is good! Just ask Him to it and He will.

Hopefully, I've convinced you if you were not already, that praying in other tongues is a very necessary part of our prayer life. But when do we pray in tongues? *Romans 8:14* says that "we are sons of God when we are led by the Spirit of God". Learning to be lead by the Spirit will enhance our prayer life and help us know when to pray in our prayer language, and when not to pray. The key is to continually yield ourselves to the promptings of the Spirit.

Ephesians 6:18
"Praying always with all prayer and supplication in the Spirit, and watching thereunto with all perseverance and supplication for all the saints"

Before we get into specific times to pray in other tongues, I want to define the term "praying in the spirit".

Praying in other tongues is not the only way to "pray in the Spirit" as some have taught. First of all, the word "spirit" is the Gr. word "*pneuma*" which means "a current of air, i.e. breath (blast) or a breeze; fig. A spirit; a prim. Root; to prostrate oneself (in homage) - fall down; Christ's spirit, divine; the Holy Ghost, life, spirit and mind

I know this is a "mouth-full", so we'll simplify it. "Praying in the Spirit" could be defined as praying with God's energy and revelation of how to pray in any given situation; being conscious of God's Spirit breathing on you. It could also be defined as "prayer that has been energized by God's Spirit".

In the Book of John we get more insight to our *motivations* as we pray in the Spirit.

<u>John 16:13</u>
"Howbeit, when He, the Spirit of Truth is come, He will guide you into all the truth, for He shall not speak of Himself, but whatsoever He shall hear, that shall He speak, and He will show you things to come. He shall glorify me"

Paul teaches us in <u>1 Cor. 14:16</u> that we are "giving thanks well" and "blessing with the spirit" when we pray in other tongues. The context in that passage of Scripture is not telling us to "forgo" praying in our own private prayer language as some have taught, but not to do it in front of people because they do not understand what you are saying; it's for our own private use.

That's one of the beautiful things about the Holy Spirit. He seeks to bring blessing to others, not confusion.

Ok. That kind of helps I hope! If I've convinced you of the need for the Baptism of the Holy Spirit with the evidence of speaking in tongues, when should we pray in our prayer languages?

Paul instructs us to "pray at all times in the Spirit". Praying in tongues is one way to "pray in the Spirit" Praying in tongues with the understanding is also another way we "pray in the Spirit". Prophesying the mind and heart of God as we are lead by the Spirit is another way of "praying in the Spirit". Some people call this "prophetic declaration". What makes it powerful is that it is energized by the Holy Spirit. Elijah didn't just decide on a whim to pray for rain. The Holy Spirit led him to pray for rain at the appointed time of God's choosing. That's one of the reasons why God answered his prayer. Elijah wasn't praying in other tongues, but was indeed "praying in the Spirit"!

When Paul exhorts us to pray at all *times*, it's the Gr. word "*kairos*" we discussed earlier in the book, meaning "set or proper times, an occasion." It implies praying at strategic times, appointed times and seasons of God. It implies times when God can intervene in people's lives by our prayers. God knows people's hearts and He knows when the enemy is going to attack. One of those strategic times was the time I shared with you when my daughter almost drowned in the Gulf of Mexico. Another time was when my oldest son had run away from home the first time after his father had left us. The enemy saw a very vulnerable child and was trying to kill him. I stayed up praying for two nights in the Spirit for him. Two days later, he returned home after police found him sleeping on a park bench, unscathed and living off of potato chips and pop! He said he was trying to teach his dad a lesson for leaving us! He can tell you stories of how

God kept him many times and believes it was because of the prayers of his mom. I don't say this with any kind of pride whatsoever, because I fell short so many times, but the Holy Spirit never stopped helping me; and as I shared in the last chapter, God has empowered me to continue praying for him. I believe today even though there is still much to be done; he is living proof that strategic prayer is necessary to keep people from totally being destroyed by the devil.

The only way we will be able to discern how to pray during those strategic times is to walk closely with the Holy Spirit and learn to recognize His voice. We always need to be ready to intercede on behalf of our loved ones and those He puts on our hearts.

Praying in other tongues is a wonderful gift that brings great benefit to a believer's life. I have summarized a few reasons why we should pray in other tongues daily as an "edification" exercise. They are as follows:

(1) To build up our spirits.
(2) To keep us aligned with the will of God.
(3) To help us pray for things we do not know about.
(4) To keep us pure and spotless . . . because when we pray in other tongues, God begins to show us our true spiritual condition
(5) To keep us refreshed and expressing our "language of thanksgiving".
(6) To bring our speech in subjection to the Spirit of God.

Twelve

Joy Comes in the Morning – Breakthrough!

In the Book of Micah we find out that God is the God of our Breakthroughs!

Micah 2:13

The One who breaks open will come up before them; they will breakout, pass through the gate, and go out by it; their King will pass before them with the LORD at their head.

Many Intercessors and Prophets have labeled this "the Breaker Anointing". In other words, when our prayers have gone up and reached critical mass, so to speak, breakthroughs are on their way whether we feel they are coming or not! That is why it is so important to stay in faith and never give up!

Breakthrough – An offensive thrust that penetrates and carries beyond a defensive line in warfare; sudden advance in knowledge or technique, moving through an obstruction; to disrupt the continuity or flow of an old system; bring it to an end or bring something *new*.

Psalms 30:5

"For His anger endureth but for a moment; in His favor is life; weeping may endure for a night, but joy cometh in the morning."

It's very interesting that it is said of the kingdom of God that it "consist of Righteousness, Peace and Joy in the Holy Spirit." (Romans 14:7) Many of us reading this have not experienced real joy in a long time because of too many oppressive situations, brokenness and loss; but I'm telling you to hang on; Morning Light is coming, and along with it the Joy of the Lord, inexpressible and full of glory! (*1 Peter 1:8*)

I love this promise in the Word of God. It shows us everything we need to know about God's faithfulness to turn our darkness into light and our mourning into joy (*Isaiah 61:3*). The only problem is that many of us didn't understand the process (*work of prayer*) that was needed to birth it! Our God is faithful to His promises to those who can and will continue to believe!

Eccl. 3:11
God makes all things beautiful in His time . . .

Beautiful - *Heb. yapheh* - good and excellent; fair and pleasant; has the connotation of being an *appropriate time.*

Appropriate - *Webster's* - especially suitable or compatible; fitting

We have to remember that God has an *"especially suitable or compatible"* time for the fulfillment of His plans for us and those we pray for whether it be for our families, our churches or our nation. I learned to trust in this principle after having to endure long seasons of prayer for my now adult *children* and I still haven't come into my fullness yet, but I continue to believe and ask God for more grace when I feel I'm lacking! We must never give up. We also need to understand that when we pray for others, there are more variables that have to be considered and worked out in each situation and only God knows what is needed to bring those prayers to fruition.

One night while praying for my children the Lord instructed me to read the following passage in the Book of Luke. I really needed the Lord's attention on some things and it seemed like they were never going to happen. After years of dealing with some of the same problems, with little or no changes, I became very discouraged, but thank God He's so patient with me. He taught me some new things that night about my faith and for that I was so grateful.

<u>Luke 18:1 & 7</u>

Then He spoke a parable to them that men always ought to pray and not lose heart saying: "There was in a certain city a judge who did not fear God nor regard man. Now there was a widow in that city; and she came to him saying, 'Get justice for me from my adversary'. And he would not for a while; but afterward He said within himself, 'though I do not fear God nor regard man, yet because this widow troubles me I will avenge her, lest by her continual coming she weary me'" Then the Lord said, "*hear*" what the unjust judge said.

Hear - *Heb. Shamah* - to hear, listen and obey; to hear with a renewed interest.

Think about that last sentence we just read! The Lord mentions in that passage for us to "hear" what the unjust judge said. It's always good to remember that there are things we've read before that somehow could have been forgotten and we need to read them again with a "renewed interest" in order to recover those hidden and very valuable secrets that could possibly hold our breakthroughs!

Luke 18:7, 8

"And shall not God avenge his own elect who cry out day and night to Him, though He bears long with them? I tell you He will avenge them speedily. Nevertheless, when the Son of Man comes, will He really find faith on the earth?"

That was really eye-opening to me because I had never really read it through with any understanding until it actually applied to my situation. I felt like that woman and I also felt like God was not hearing me. If you've ever prayed for your children, for instance, to come to the Lord and years have passed with no answered prayer, you will understand the frustration I felt.

In that example, the Lord was teaching me to continue coming to Him until I received my answers. Many people call this the prayer of "*importunity*" which is also *intercession*.

Importunity - *Webster's* - persistent; especially to the point of annoyance or intrusion

Wow! The truths of that passage, coupled with the definition of that word began to change my paradigm about how I viewed *intercessory prayer*! I asked myself over and over, am I reading this correctly? God wants us to annoy Him? Is that unbelief to continually go to God and ask over and over for the same thing, especially if these situations were sometimes very urgent and in need of God's attention?

Obviously it's not unbelief, especially from the gleanings of this passage; He wants us to be *persistent* until we see it done!

Persistent – *Webster's* – continue firmly or obstinately in an opinion or course of action in spite of difficulty, opposition, or failure.

This was yet another wow moment for me! Then came the questions, how long God – I knew in my heart what His answer would be; until your faith becomes sight! What do I do until it's done? Before we go any further, I want us to look at the last thing He said in that Parable; "Nevertheless, when the Son of Man comes, will He really find *faith* on the earth?" (*vs.* 7) The light bulb came on for sure. He was not only talking about being persistent in prayer or "working the word" as I've heard some say, but it was also a matter of pressing on and making our *faith* strong in spite of "difficulty, opposition, or failure."

Hebrews 11:1 & 6
"Now faith is the substance of things hoped for, the evidence of things not seen."
"But without faith it is impossible to please Him, for He who comes to God must believe that He is, and that He is a rewarder of them that diligent seek Him."

Here we see that God not only requires *faith* but *rewards* it. Look at God's own words to Abraham recorded in the Book of Genesis.

Genesis 15:1
"After these things the word of the LORD came to Abram in a vision, saying, 'Do not be afraid, Abram. I am your exceedingly great reward.'"

Reward – *Heb. Sakar* – payment of a contract; salary, wages; by implication, compensation, benefit

In essence God said to Abraham, don't be afraid to believe me – even though it may take more time than you realize, I'll make it well worth your while to give you what you ask for. Nothing is impossible to them that continue to believe. With promises like these in the word of God, giving up should never be an option!

<u>Gal. 6:9</u>
"And let us not grow weary while doing well, for in due season we shall reap if we do not lose heart."

This passage shows us another gold nugget or *secret to breaking through in prayer*. Never give up on someone you are praying for or for your bad situations to turn around. Find promises in the word of God for your situation and begin to speak them forth to encourage you in the building of your faith. Faith is the force by which we obtain all of the "precious promises". God is faithful and He's working it out in His time, but I can hear some of you saying, 'what if I'm past all of that time and I've totally given up?' There is still *hope*!

One day while preparing a message for our television program "Hope for Your Future" I decided to take a break. I turned the television on to see what was going on in the world. There was a commercial running for a Cancer Hospital in Tulsa, OK. Their motto was "Hope is your Mainstay". At first this didn't mean anything to me because I hadn't really understood how important it was to have hope. Then as I thought about it, I couldn't let go of the word "mainstay". Looking it up in the dictionary proved to be a valuable expansion of my understated definition of hope.

Hope – *Webster's* – To desire with expectation of obtainment; to expect with confidence

Mainstay – *Webster's* – a very important part of something; something or someone that provides support and makes it possible for something to exist or succeed

Our hope becomes an invaluable source of strength and *support* as we are building our faith in order to obtain those things we pray for.

<u>Hebrews 6:19</u>
"Hope is the anchor of our souls . . ."

Anchor – *Agkyra* – Metaphor for any stay or safeguard

In other words, hope keeps us anchored into the promises of God! It acts as a pillar or an unseen force that holds us up in preparation to receive whatever is needed for healing or restoration. (*Again, I refer to my book "The Scent of Water" Hope and Healing for Relationships*)

Even during the Apostasy of Jeremiah's day I shared in the earlier chapters of this book, and the shocking reality of how closely related to their times we are in our nation today, God still offers us hope as He did to them.

<u>Jeremiah 29:11</u>
For I know the plans I have for you, declares the Lord. They are plans for good and not for disaster, to give you a future and a "HOPE".

Yes, conditions have to be met, intercession and repentance must come forth, but hope is the mainstay to keep us confident that better days are ahead for all who will permit it!

I'm sure by now many of you have heard the term "Hope Deferred Makes the Heart Sick". Unfortunately, many of you that have picked up this book are in what the Bible calls a "hope deferred" state of mind and have totally given up.

<u>Proverbs 13:12</u>
"Hope deferred maketh the heart sick; but a desire fulfilled is a tree of life."

Deferred - *Heb. Mashak* - draw or drag along; draw out; prolong

You may not even have any hope right now, much less be in faith due to so many negative circumstances that have caused brokenness and loss in your life. I want you to know that your hope can be restored; you can get up and get out of that pit you're in, and retrieve your faith in order to possess God's promises. Many times our faith is lost during battles we were never prepared to face. Staying hopeless in the pit is not an option we can afford to choose.

The loss of hope will not only hinder your progress and keep you from being able to retrieve your promises from God by faith, but will also cause you to become *sick*.

Sick - *Heb. Chalah* - to be or become weak; to be or become sick or diseased; be or become grieved to the point of death; to be or become sorrowful with no hope or relief

When someone is suffering from hope deferred they are at a very serious disadvantage with the devil until they are willing to deal with it!

In my book "The Scent of Water" Hope and Healing for Relationships, I've written an entire chapter on this condition known as "*hope deferred*" because many of my clients were suffering from it; I myself suffered for over seven (7) years with that same condition prior to God healing me. People in this category have just given up and don't even know how to approach God anymore. It's not that they don't believe in God or His promises but they get overwhelmed in situations seemingly out of their control. For instance: an unexpected divorce, abuse, children on drugs, death of loved ones, loss of income, sudden illnesses etc. Listen, we all know life is hard, but the devil does his best to try and hide the truth that God is still GOOD. He hides this truth from Christians and Non-Christians alike and because of it; they have lost all hope for their future. The enemy has no favorites but does his best work when we are unaware of his devices.

Let's look at it again:

Proverbs 13:12
"*Hope deferred* makes the heart sick; but when the desire comes, it is a tree of *life*."

Yes, absolutely there will be those times when prayers seemingly go unanswered and you and I might be tempted to get discouraged. Just in case you haven't noticed, life is still going on when you've lost hope and more weapons are being aimed at us by the enemy to attack in those vulnerable areas. The Apostle Peter warned us about this in the following passage of Scripture.

<u>1 Peter 5:8</u>
Be sober be vigilant; because your adversary the devil walk about like a roaring lion, seeking whom he may devour.

Sober - Gr. *Nepho* - be calm and collected in spirit;

Vigilant - Gr. *Gregoreo* - to be watchful; *metaphor* - give strict attention to; in order to ward off some destructive calamity that could suddenly overtake someone.

This is not meant to scare anyone or make light of the extreme circumstances any of us are presently suffering from, but to recognize the way out. We are not alone. Jesus told us that we have a very slick and calculated enemy that, by the way, has already been defeated for us.

<u>John 16:33</u>
These things I have already spoken unto you, that in Me you might have peace. In the world ye shall have tribulation: but be of good cheer; I have overcome the world.

<u>Philippians 4:6 - 8</u>
"Be anxious for nothing; but in everything by *prayer* and *supplication* with *thanksgiving* let your request be made known unto God; And the peace of the God which passes all understanding, shall keep your hearts and minds through Christ Jesus."

When we get stuck in "hope deferred" for any period of time, the enemy gains an advantage he should have never gotten! That's when the devil is at work against us because he recognizes our weakness and inability to rise up and pray. Some of this is self pity of course, and self pity leads to "hope deferred" and becomes a catalyst for sickness, disease and all kinds of other problems we are not able to deal with.

Ask me how I found this out! We are all inclined to feel sorry for ourselves when we are hurt or feel deprived or victimized. The enemy knows this. We have to realize that we can't stay in the pit of self pity or we will lose our battles. Our God is on our side and offers a way out of the mess and the depression that feeds it! Acknowledging it is the first step!

This is not negative news. This is reality. We are in a fight and have to stay close to God. Sometimes there will be long seasons of waiting on the Lord to do what He's promised; that will give us plenty of time to lose our hope, unless we do stay close to Him.

Sarah and Abraham waited almost twenty-five (25) years before the fruition of their promise! We know he had to have hope!

Think about all the cruel things done to Joseph: His brothers wanting to kill him at age 17 and instead sold him into slavery; He was purchased by Potiphar, one of Pharaoh's officials, and served as a house slave for approximately 11 years; was falsely accused of trying to seduce Potiphar's wife that landed him in prison for approximately 2 more years! Scriptures tell us at that time "the Lord was with Joseph" (*another secret of breakthrough*) and one we must tell ourselves daily while praying and believing! It wasn't until he was 39 years old that he was finally promoted and made Overseer, 2nd in command to Pharaoh's Kingdom and restored to his father and brothers! (*Genesis 39:21*) He will also do that for us if we believe!

Remember, hope is vital to our recovery in our families, our churches and our nation. We must embrace it and let it propel us towards a tried and purified faith in order to receive God's promises.

If we have no hope, we will not pray. If we will not pray, we will not release life to those who need our prayers! Sometimes prayer is simply speaking by revelation what God says. Since God's Spirit is a life-giving Spirit and He lives in us by His Spirit, when we pray or speak, we are able to release God's life-giving words for those in need. Look at the following powerful Scriptures that reveal these truths.

Proverbs 18:21
"Death and life are in the power of the tongue; and they that love it shall eat the fruit thereof."

John 6:63
"It is the spirit who gives life; the flesh profits nothing. The words that I speak to you are spirit and they are life."

Definitions:

Life – *Heb. Chay* – alive; living; revival of life

Spirit – Gr. – *Pneuma* – Spirit of God; breath

Life – Gr. – *Zoe* – the life which comes from or belongs to God; God's life

Through prayer we release that which is "necessary to sustain life" in all situations we are burdened to pray for. We have the ability to speak *life* through our prayers. Remember the words God gave me when my son had that horrible accident? God spoke by revelation in my heart the following two powerful passages of Scripture that were vital – necessary to sustain life - while standing in front of that police officer in the foyer of our office building:

Genesis 50:20
"What Satan has meant for harm, God will turn it around and use it for good to save many people"

Psalms 118:17
"He will live and not die and declare the glory of the Lord"

Upon arrival at the hospital, much to my amazement, God had people in place who were speaking "life giving words" over my precious son with the same passage of Scripture, "He will live and not die and declare the glory of the Lord". God had people in place, totally unaware to me, to provide help in supporting me in this incredible battle!

This is why our hope is so very important to maintain. To lose our hope causes us to [1]forfeit the promises of God [2]create serious conflict within us and [3]make us sick over time.

We must continue to believe that God hears our prayers no matter how long it takes. He's the One who gives us the breakthroughs we need! We have to change our *perspective* or we risk getting into a serious disadvantage in the battles we face.

Perspective – *Webster's* – a way of looking at or thinking about something

King David verified this truth in the Book of Psalms:

<u>*Psalms 27:13 – 14*</u>
"I would have lost heart and *fainted* unless I believed that I would see the goodness of the Lord in the land of the living."

Fainted is a word that is pretty close to the *Heb.* word *sick.*

Fainted – *Heb. Puwg* – to grow numb; feeble (weak & sickly) to be void of vital warmth

Notice he said that this would have happened to him if he hadn't continued to believe in spite of all the troubles he went through. We must keep hope alive! Don't stop believing!

The "Breaker" will come through for us and we will see the Morning Light and be filled with joy unspeakable and full of Glory at the fulfillment of the promise!

ABOUT THE AUTHOR

Donna Sundberg is a 1991 graduate of Rhema Bible Training Center in Broken Arrow, OK, and is licensed and ordained through the Federations of Ministers and Churches, Int'l located in Cedar Hills, TX. She is married and has three (3) children and three (3) grandchildren.

Her desire is to see people born into the Kingdom of God and come to a full revelation of the Holy Spirit and His place in helping us accomplish God's plan for our lives. She has served faithfully in many churches and in particular, Women's Ministry under several pastoral teams; Women's Aglow Boards in Louisiana over a period of ten (10) years; taught children in two Christian schools and served as a Chaplain in a Christian School in Garland, TX. She has traveled extensively in the Evangelistic/Teaching ministry throughout the South, Midwest and Mexico, and has helped co-pastor three (3) churches with her husband, expanding over twenty-three (23) years. She and her husband initiated a mobile training school (SCM School of Ministry) that trains and equips the Body of Christ in their unique gifts and callings. After serving 15 years as a Biblical Relationship Consultant she founded By God's Design – *Healing Workshops for Life* – where she teaches on Behavioral, Emotional and Relational Issues as they pertain to health.

The Holy Spirit has used her in His gifts as she travels in the ministry. These gifts include, but or not limited to, prophetic teaching and preaching, gifts of healings, prophetic songs, word of knowledge, word of wisdom, and prophecy.

Signs, wonders, and healings truly follow this vessel as she places total dependency upon the Lord she serves, and His Spirit's power to perform the works of God. She and her husband reside in Dallas, TX.

RESOURCES

Scripture References:

All Scripture References taken from the KJV or NKJV Exhaustive Concordance of the Bible and Strong's Exhaustive Concordance of the Bible: Thomas Nelson Publishers, 1990, unless otherwise noted.

Books and Study Aids:

Bounds, E.M., Prayer and Praying Men, Grand Rapides, MI: Baker Book House, 1991

Hagin, Kenneth E., The Art of Intercession, U.S.: Rhema Bible Church, A.K.A. Kenneth Hagin Ministries, 1980

Kemble, Traci, The Courage to Say No More, ISBN 0-9654133-1-4, U.S: Elijah Productions and Publishing 1995

Merriam-Webster, The Merriam-Webster Dictionary, Springfield, MA: Merriam-Webster Inc., 1997

Others not listed here are mentioned throughout the book.

DONNA B. SUNDBERG

Call or write:

Sundberg Christian Ministries, Inc.
P.O. Box 801402
Dallas, TX 75380
Ph. 405.659.3964

Please visit our website:
www.SCMonline.org

She is available for Evangelistic Meetings,
Conferences, Workshops and Seminars